MILESTONES
IN MODERN WORLD HISTORY

The Treaty of Nanking

MILESTONES
IN MODERN
WORLD HISTORY

MILESTONES
IN MODERN WORLD HISTORY

1600 · · · 1750 ·   · · · 1940 · · · 2000

The Treaty of Nanking

DENNIS ABRAMS

CHELSEA HOUSE
An Infobase Learning Company

The Treaty of Nanking

Copyright © 2011 by Infobase Learning

Chelsea House
An imprint of Infobase Learning
132 West 31st Street
New York, NY 10001

Library of Congress Cataloging-in-Publication Data

Abrams, Dennis, 1960–
The Treaty of Nanking / by Dennis Abrams.
 p. cm.—(Milestones in modern world history)
Includes bibliographical references and index.
ISBN 978-1-60413-495-7 (hardcover)
1. China—History—Opium War, 1840–1842—Juvenile literature. 2. China. Treaties, etc.
Great Britain, 1842 Aug. 29—Juvenile literature. 3. China—Foreign relations—Great Brit-
ain—Juvenile literature. 4. Great Britain—Foreign relations—China—Juvenile literature. I.
Title. II. Series.

DS757.5.A24 2011
951'.033—dc22   2010026903

Text design by Erik Lindstrom
Cover design by Alicia Post
Composition by Keith Trego
Cover printed by Bang Printing, Brainerd, Minn.
Book printed and bound by Bang Printing, Brainerd, Minn.
Date printed: March 2011
Printed in the United States of America

10 9 8 7 6 5 4 3 2 1

This book is printed on acid-free paper.

CONTENTS

Two Worlds Collide

The year was 1792. George III was king of England, and Qianlong was the emperor of China. The two great nations had no formal diplomatic relationship. Indeed, China had no formal diplomatic relationship with any other nation. In the eyes of the Chinese, all other nations were "barbarians," unworthy of being treated as equals.

The economic ties between England and China were growing, though, as China began selling greater and greater amounts of tea to England. Thus, King George III made the decision that the time had come to establish a new level of relationship with China, sending as his emissary Lord George Macartney.

Lord Macartney, the son of a down-on-his-luck Irish gentleman, had achieved much in his short career. After studying law in London, he quickly made himself known in political circles and received a knighthood. At the age of just 27, he had been sent as Envoy Extraordinary to the Russian court of Empress Catherine the Great. After achieving success there, he returned to London, where he was elevated to the Irish peerage and was sent in 1780 to rule the Indian state of Madras. That mission was also a success, so sending him to China as the first official British ambassador to that kingdom seemed to be the logical progression in what had heretofore been a brilliant career.

The delegation sent to China reflected the importance placed on the mission by the British government. Lord Macartney sailed on a newly manufactured man-of-war equipped with 66 guns that was flanked by two support ships. Each of these ships was laden with gifts specially selected to shock and awe the Chinese with the finest that British manu-facturing technology could achieve, including telescopes, globes, clocks, musical instruments, carriages—even a hot-air balloon complete with a man fully trained to fly it. Lord Macartney was also accompanied by an entourage of nearly 100 of England's best, including artists, scientists, guards, valets, and Chinese-language teachers.

The trip was a long one. After leaving London in September 1792, it was not until June 1793 that Macartney arrived in China, stopping briefly in the port city of Canton (today known as Guangzhou). From there, the delegation's representatives were permitted to go directly to Tianjin and land there, based on their somewhat dubious claim that they had come to honor the emperor on his eightieth birthday.

On August 6, Macartney went ashore in Tientsen (today known as Tianjin) to meet the viceroy of Pechili. The viceroy informed Macartney that the emperor, who had ruled China for 57 years, had left Peking—known today as Beijing—but would be pleased to grant the delegation an audience at his hunting lodge at Jenol (today known as Chengde). The heavier gifts were put ashore, and the rest of the delegation

The Irish diplomat Lord George Macartney, as he appeared on the cover of *European Magazine* in 1796. Macartney became Britain's first ambassador to China in 1793.

moved to a Chinese fleet of small wooden boats, called junks and sampans.

An interesting historical note is that Qianlong later observed that the gifts were suitable only for the amusement of children. Even the spring-suspension coach was dismissed as impossible for the emperor to use, because Qianlong could never "suffer any man to sit higher than himself, and to turn his back towards him."[1] Seventy years later, when British and French troops destroyed the Summer Palace, the gifts were discovered, still unused, in a stable.

On the mast of Lord Macartney's houseboat was a flag, inscribed with Chinese characters, easily read by any literate Chinese that said, "*Tribute from the Red Barbarians.*" It was not an auspicious beginning. On September 14, 1793, Lord Macartney, garbed in the mantle of the Knight of the Bath, over a suit of speckled mulberry velvet, finally presented himself to the Chinese emperor. He was accompanied by Sir George Staunton and Staunton's 12-year-old son, George, as their page. The emperor, determined to make it clear to the British that he was not participating in a meeting of equals but in a meeting with foreign barbarians, met the delegation not in the formal surroundings of his palace, but in a yurt—a primitive horsehair tent used by nomadic horsemen. The message and insult to the British could not have been clearer. They were not worthy of being treated as the emperor's equal.

Traditionally, "barbarian" envoys to China who were brought into the presence of the emperor were required to kowtow to show their respect: Kneeling from a standing position three times, each time bowing low enough to touch their heads against the floor. This was too much for Lord Macartney, who made it clear that he would bow down on one knee to the emperor, just as he would for King George, but would not, under any circumstances, kowtow to the emperor. Just this once, the emperor of the Celestial Empire decided to allow the barbarian's lack of courtesy and respect to pass.

In 1793, Lord George Macartney led the first British embassy to Imperial China but refused to kowtow before the emperor. Emperor Qianlong met the British delegation in a primitive horsehair tent called a yurt to show that he did not believe the British were his equals.

After the ceremonial bowing was completed, Lord Macartney presented to the emperor a personal letter from King George III enclosed in a gold box covered with diamonds. He then gave the emperor his list of requests: the right for the British to maintain a diplomatic residence in the Chinese capital of Peking (today known as Beijing); an easing of trading restrictions; and the opening of new ports for international commerce, since at the time, foreigners were allowed to trade only in the city of Canton and only under heavily circumscribed conditions. After hearing out the king's envoy, the emperor and his minister politely said no to all of the requests.

Instead, Emperor Qianlong sent an edict to George III, explaining in the most patient and courteous of terms that the Chinese were not interested in either increasing foreign commerce *or* in establishing diplomatic relations with the British. The letter said in part:

> I do not forget the lonely remoteness of your island, cut off from the world by intervening wastes of sea, nor do I overlook your excusable ignorance of the usages of Our Celestial Empire. . . .[2]
>
> Our ways have no resemblance to yours, and even were your envoy competent to acquire some rudiments of them, he could not transplant them to your barbarous land. Strange and costly objects do not interest me.[3]

The Chinese emperor went on to say to the British king:

> We have never valued ingenious articles, nor do we have the slightest need of your country's manufactures. Therefore, O King, as regards your request to send someone to remain at the capital, while it is not in harmony with the regulations of the Celestial Empire, we also feel very much that it is of no advantage to your country.[4]

The carefully composed note had, in fact, been written on July 30, more than six weeks before the British diplomats had even met the emperor. The meeting itself had been a useless exercise. There was nothing left for Macartney to say or do in response. He returned to Canton by the land route and sailed back to England. He wrote in his journal: "The Empire of China is an old, crazy, first rate man-of-war, which a fortunate succession of able and vigilant officers has contrived to keep afloat for these one hundred and fifty years past, and to overawe their neighbors merely by her bulk and appearance."[5] He went on to add that, ultimately, China's resistance to British goals was futile. While Macartney's prediction came true, it would be 23 years before the British tried sending another ambassador to China.

ANOTHER TRY

It took nearly that long for the Chinese themselves to recover from the indignities of Macartney's visit. The Chinese mandarins—the bureaucrats of imperial China—were troubled over what to do about the "barbarian" envoy's refusal to kowtow to the emperor. In an attempt not to set a bad example for other envoys to follow, and in order to make things easier for themselves, they simply falsified the record to indicate that Lord Macartney had indeed kowtowed to the emperor, "thus acknowledging that Great Britain was a far-off country subordinate to China."[6] By the time the next British envoy— William Pitt, Lord Amherst—arrived in 1816, however, it was decided that there would be no more falsifying of the records. This envoy *would* kowtow to the current emperor, Jiaqing, the fifteenth son of Qianlong.

Lord Amherst was advised on his mission by George Staunton, the chairman of the East India Company's Select Committee in Canton and a respected businessman and Chinese scholar. He was the very same George Staunton who had served as page for Lord Macartney's mission to China in 1793. Staunton told Lord Amherst in no uncertain terms that he should *not* kowtow to the emperor. Doing so would show the Chinese that the British were indeed unequal and knew it, which would then make them unworthy of engaging in any real discussion in the eyes of the Chinese.

Not surprisingly, the meeting was a fiasco bordering on farce. Immediately upon his arrival in China, Lord Amherst was asked by Chinese authorities to show his respect for the emperor by kowtowing, without a large audience, to the emperor's empty throne. Amherst, though, made it clear to the mandarins that he would give nine bows, even on bended knee, to the emperor's throne, but nothing more. The mandarins, though, were still determined that *this* envoy would show the proper respect to the emperor. Since their polite request did not work, they would have to rely on stealth and tricks to make it happen.

KOWTOW

Illustrious representatives of the British throne such as Lord Macartney and Lord Amherst refused to kowtow (to kneel and touch one's forehead to the floor) to the emperor, believing that it would show them, and by extension their sovereign, humbling themselves to Chinese authority. To the Chinese people, however, the act of kowtowing was an act of respect, and the highest sign of reverence. Kowtowing was widely used to show reverence not just to the emperor, but also to one's elders and superiors, as well as for religious and cultural objects of worship.

It is interesting to note that there were several grades of kowtow that could be used, depending on the solemnity of the situation. In the most solemn of ceremonies—the coronation of a new emperor, for example—the emperor's subject would take part in the ceremony of the "three kneelings and nine kowtows." This involved kneeling from a standing position three times; and each time one kneeled, performing the kowtow three times. In most instances, though, a single kowtow was sufficient to show proper respect.

Amherst, exhausted from his long trip to China, was quickly separated from his luggage and most of his retinue and hurried through the night to the emperor's Summer Palace, where he was scheduled to meet the emperor at dawn. There, if he would not kowtow on his own, the mandarins were certain that a good shove of the exhausted envoy would send him sprawling onto the floor—the closest to a proper kowtow they felt they could get out of the stubborn Englishman.

In addition, since government officials represented the power of the emperor while carrying out their duties, commoners were required to kowtow to them in formal situations. A commoner, for example, when brought before a magistrate, would be required to kneel and kowtow. He would then be required to remain kneeling, while a person of higher status, such as one who had earned a degree in the imperial examinations, would be permitted to take a seat.

Since Confucian philosophy required that one showed great reverence to one's parents and grandparents, children were required to kowtow to their elderly ancestors, particularly on special occasions. At a wedding, for example, the marrying couple was traditionally required to kowtow to both sets of parents, as an acknowledgment of the debt they were owed for their role as parents.

Today, of course, the kowtow has largely disappeared, replaced with a simple standing bow as a sign of respect. The tradition, however, remains in some instances. Some Chinese still kowtow before the grave of an ancestor, while some couples still kowtow toward their parents during a wedding. Chinese martial arts schools often require a student to kowtow toward their instructor, and traditional performing arts also require the kowtow.

Despite the mandarins' best efforts, however, Lord Amherst managed to remain upright. There would be no kowtowing to Emperor Jiaqing. That was both the beginning and end of Lord Amherst's trip to China. The meeting was called to a close, and Lord Amherst was unceremoniously expelled from the country. Obviously, the British and Chinese were no closer to establishing any kind of diplomatic relationship than they had been 23 years earlier, and the two lands were no closer to understanding each other than they had ever been.

DIFFERENT WORLDS

The problem remained that Great Britain and China were two countries with very different aims, as well as very different ideas about their nation and its place in the world. The goal and reason for the existence of the British Empire was to expand its territorial control and its trade throughout the world, and to dominate the world economically.

China, on the other hand, already felt that it was the center of the world. Its leaders believed that because the outside world was filled with "barbarians," it had nothing to offer the Chinese that they did not already have themselves. Other nations could come to China to show their respect to the emperor and his land, but nothing more. With one world wanting to expand its contacts throughout the world, and the other world supremely uninterested in any outside contacts with anyone, it is little wonder that the two nations were unable to even come close to understanding each other's goals.

There was, though, one item that the two nations had reached a modicum of understanding over: tea. The Chinese, who grew large amounts of quality tea, were interested in selling it to the British, who were rapidly developing an all-consuming thirst for the leafy product. There was one problem though. The British did not want to spend actual money on tea. They wanted, instead, to trade with the Chinese and offered them a product they had in exchange for the highest quality tea then grown in the world.

What, then, would the Chinese need from the British? As an Englishman of the time pointed out, "The Chinese have the best food in the world, rice; the best drink, tea; and the best clothing, cotton, silk, and fur. . . . They do not need to buy a cent's worth elsewhere."[7] After several attempts at finding something, *anything*, to trade with the Chinese, a product was finally found. It was a product grown in large amounts in the area around the town of Ghazipur, in the north Indian state of Uttar Pradesh, a land already under British control. The product was opium—a narcotic with addictive properties that guaranteed a constant demand.

It was through the sale of opium that the British worked to open up China to foreign trade. The sale of opium also led to increasing tension between the two nations, ultimately culminating in a war between these two very different nations. Finally, it was through opium that a treaty was signed that forever changed China and its relationship to the world.

Before we can tell the story of the opium war, however, we need to go back further in time. We need to understand how Britain and China reached the starting point at which our history of the Treaty of Nanking begins. We will begin by looking at the Celestial Empire—China.

The Celestial Kingdom

In the year A.D. 1600, the empire of China was the largest and most sophisticated of all the unified realms on earth. The extent of its territorial domains was unparalleled at a time when Russia was only just beginning to coalesce as a country, India was fragmented between Mughal and Hindu rulers, and a grim combination of infectious disease and Spanish conquerors had laid low the once great empires of Mexico and Peru. And China's population of some 120 million was far larger than that of all the European countries combined.[1]

No other country on Earth could compete with China when it came to pomp, ritual, or even something such as the sheer size of the ruler's palace. In Peking, the emperor of China lived in the enormous palace complex known as the

Forbidden City. With its yellow roofs and marble courts, laid out in carefully planned geometric order, the Forbidden City had doors and stairways of each palace building and throne hall that were aligned with the arches that led out of Peking in the south. This precise melding of the Forbidden City with the world outside its walls demonstrated to the world "the connectedness of things personified in this man the Chinese termed the Son of Heaven."[2]

As historian Jonathan D. Spence points out in *The Search for Modern China*, "In the late sixteenth century the Ming dynasty seemed at the height of its glory."[3] Ruling China since 1368, the Ming "created one of the greatest eras of orderly government and social stability in human history."[4] Under Ming rule, culture and the arts thrived, and the economy blossomed, helping prosperity to increase among nearly all Chinese. In addition, Chinese accomplishments in printing and the manufacture of such items as silk and porcelain were unrivaled by anything being done in Europe at the same time. This period of Chinese glory, however, was soon to end.

The economy began to falter, which led to lower tax revenues, which in turn led to the government's inability to pay its army in a timely manner. This, then, led to troop desertions, which encouraged outsiders to begin pushing against Chinese borders. Inadequate government attention and poor weather led to a series of bad crops, which led to starvation, disease, and death on a wide scale among the increasingly restless and unhappy rural population.

As one Chinese historian wrote of the Zhejiang province in 1642,

> the symptoms of pestilence rose again on a large scale, affecting eight or nine out of every ten households. It even reached the point where in a household of ten or twenty people a single uninfected person could not be found, or where in such a household there was not one saved. Therefore at

first the bodies were buried in coffins, and next in grasses, but finally they were left on the beds.[5]

With this combination of factors, it is little wonder that the Ming dynasty began to face revolts from within and armed invasions from the outside. In April 1644, one of the leading rebels, Li Zicheng, attacked Peking with an army of hundreds of thousands of discontented Chinese citizens; his armies entered Peking without a fight. On learning that the rebels had entered the city, Emperor Chongzhen, safe behind the walls of the Forbidden City, called for his government ministers to meet with him the following morning so that he could hear their advice. (That evening, according to records, the drunken emperor murdered one of his wives and cut off the right arm of his daughter, Princess Chanping.)

The next day though, when none of his ministers appeared (they had all fled upon hearing of the rebels' entry into Peking), the emperor walked alone to the imperial garden located just outside of the walls of the Forbidden City, the 7,800,000-square-foot (724,643.7-square-meter) palace complex his family had built between 1406 and 1420. There, Emperor Chongzhen, who had ruled China for 17 years, hung himself from a tree next to a red pavilion that housed the Imperial Hat and Girdle Company. His body, dressed in a blue silk robe and red pants, was found three days later, along with a note bearing two Chinese characters written in his own hand: *Tian zi*—the Son of Heaven. With that, the Ming dynasty came to an end.

THE MANCHUS INVADE

Although Li Zicheng's rebel army was now in Peking, he would not establish the next dynasty to rule China. That dynasty would come from the northeast, among tribes originally known as Jurchen; today they are known as the Manchus. Well organized both militarily and administratively, the Manchus began making tentative moves into outer territories the Chinese considered part of China as early as 1610. Around 1616, the Manchu leader, Nurhaci, began pushing hard against the declining power of the Ming government.

Confident in his power and ability to lead, Nurhaci scorned Ming power, writing to one Chinese officer: "Even if you fight, you certainly will not win . . . if you do not fight, but surrender, I shall let you keep your former office and shall care benevolently for you. But if you fight, how can our arrows know who you are?"[6] In 1626, Nurhaci died, and after a brief struggle for power, his eighth son, Hong Taiji, took over the reins of power. Twelve years later, he declared the formation of a new dynasty called the Qing, which he declared would rule over both the Manchus and all neighboring peoples, including the Chinese.

Hong Taiji died in 1643 before that could happen, leaving his five-year-old son as his heir, with Hong Taiji's younger brother Dorgon as his regent—the person who would rule until the designated heir came of age. Before any Manchu could rule over China, they would have to contend, in the spring of 1644, with both the rebel leader Li Zicheng, and the last remaining major Ming general, Wu Sangui.

On June 6, the Manchus entered Peking along with their new ally, the Ming general Wu, who felt it in his best interest to side with the Manchus rather than with Li Zicheng. The new emperor took the title of Shunzhi, a word that combined the Chinese character for *Shun*, meaning "obedience," and *–zhi*, meaning "to rule." With that, the Manchus openly declared that the mandate of heaven, the right to rule China, was theirs.

Of course, declaring that you have received the mandate of heaven does not necessarily make it so. The decline of the Mings and the struggle to rule China had taken too long, had alienated too many people, and had damaged the country too

(continues on page 24)

THE GREAT WALL

A technological feat, the longest protective wall ever built, and a symbol to many of the country itself, the Great Wall of China remains one of the world's greatest landmarks and achievements. Surprisingly, the wall is not just one wall, but a series of stone and earthen fortifications built, rebuilt, and maintained between the fifth century B.C. and the sixteenth century A.D. in order to protect the northern borders of the Chinese empire from Xiongnu attacks during the rule of several successive dynasties. (The Xiongnu were a confederation of nomadic tribes from central Asia that lived on the steppes of northern China.)

One of the most famous of these walls is the wall built between 220 and 206 B.C. by the first emperor of China, Qin Shi Huang. Little of it, however, remains. Stones from the mountains were used in construction over mountain ranges, while rammed earth was used for construction in the plains. Most of these ancient walls have long since eroded away, but attempts were made to repair, rebuild, and expand parts of this section of wall during the Han, Sui, Northern, and Jin dynasties.

It would be up to the Ming dynasty to rebuild and rethink the concept of the Great Wall. After the defeat of the Ming armies by the Oirats in the Battle of Tumu in 1449, and their subsequent failure to gain the upper hand over Manchurian and Mongolian tribes, the Ming adopted a new strategy to keep the nomadic tribes out of China by constructing walls along its northern border.

Unlike the earlier Qin fortifications, however, the Ming construction was stronger and more elaborate because of the use of bricks and stone instead of rammed earth. As Mongol raids continued over the years, the Ming devoted

The Great Wall of China, a series of stone and earthen fortifications, was built to protect the northern borders of the Chinese Empire against invaders.

considerable manpower and financial resources to repair and reinforce the walls.

As the Ming dynasty began to fail, it was the Great Wall that helped to defend the empire against the Manchu invasions that began around 1600. Under the military command of Yuan Chonghuan, the Ming army held off the Manchus at the heavily fortified Shanhaiguan pass, thereby preventing the Manchus from entering the Chinese interior. The Manchus were able to cross the Great Wall only in 1644, when the gates at Shanhaiguan were opened by Wu Sangui, allowing them to proceed with their invasion and subsequent takeover of control of China. Under Manchu rule, China's borders were extended beyond that of the walls,

(continues)

(continued)

and Mongolia was made part of China, so construction and repairs on the Great Wall were discontinued.

At 4,000 miles (6,437 kilometers) long, the wall at its peak was guarded by more than one million men. It has been estimated that somewhere between 2 million and 3 million Chinese died as part of the centuries-long project of building the wall. Time and man have taken on their toll on the wall, for while some portions of the wall north of Beijing and near tourist centers have been preserved and even reconstructed, in many locations the wall is in a serious state of disrepair. In some sections, the wall is used as a village playground or as a source of material to rebuild houses and roads. Sections of the wall have been vandalized or covered with graffiti. Remarkably, parts of the wall have even been destroyed to make room for modern construction. As of this writing, no comprehensive survey of the wall has been carried out, so it is impossible to say just how much of it survives.

(continued from page 21)

much to allow for a quick, happy ending. It would take years for the new Qing dynasty to consolidate its rule over China, but consolidate they did.

CONSOLIDATION

The main architect of the Qing consolidation was the emperor Kangxi, who ruled over China from 1661 to 1722, a 61-year reign. Kangxi secured China's borders on all sides, restored the national examination system that tested all government bureaucrats, and strengthened the bureaucracy itself by improving the flow of information from throughout the country to Peking.

He also helped to heal the wounds of years of war and unite the ethnic Chinese and their Manchu rulers.

Kangxi's son, Emperor Yongzheng, worked hard to build on his father's accomplishments. Yongzheng reformed the tax system, organized the nation's cultural life, and helped to bridge the sizable gap between the nation's elite and the vast majority of the country, the rural peasants. This was a period of consolidation for China, a time of looking inward to solve the nation's internal problems and strengthen the country as a whole. The outside world, therefore, held little or no interest to China's rulers.

CHINA AND THE OUTSIDE WORLD

It has become known as the Sinocentric system. ("Sino" is a term that refers to all things related to China. For example, "sinology" is the study of Chinese history, language, and literature.) The Chinese held that the nations that surrounded China, such as Japan, Korea, and Vietnam, were mere vassals of China, countries that owed allegiance and submission to their powerful neighbor. All areas outside of this influence were called Huawaizhdi, meaning *uncivilized lands*—lands whose inhabitants were considered mere barbarians.

At the center of this system—indeed, at the center of the world—stood China, ruled by whichever dynasty could persuade its people that it had gained the Mandate of Heaven. The Celestial Empire, which the Chinese regarded as the only civilization in the world, was distinguished from the rest of the world by its codes of morality and propriety created by the philosopher Confucius. The emperor of China himself was seen as the only true emperor in the entire world. All other cultures and civilizations were by definition inferior, barbaric, and of no interest to the Chinese.

This view of China as the center of the world, as the so-called Middle Kingdom, becomes clear when one reads of a

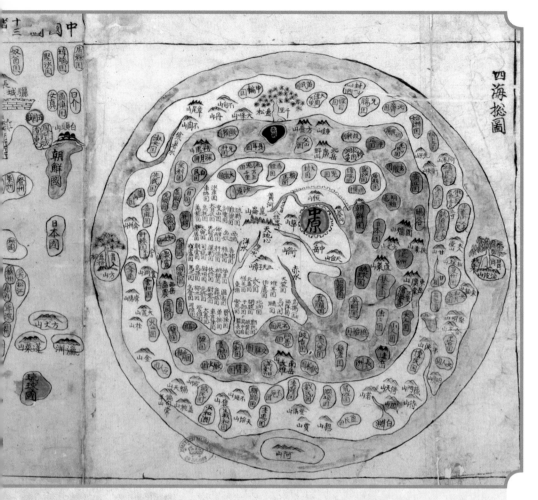

A Chinese map of the world, circa 1500. The Chinese emperor and aristocracy believed their nation was literally and figuratively the center of the world and that all other nations were by definition inferior to the Chinese Empire.

Chinese reaction to a Western map of the world, one published by Matteo Ricci, a Jesuit priest:

> Lately Matteo Ricci utilized some false teachings to fool people, and scholars unanimously believed him. . . . Take for example the position of China on the map. He puts it not in

the center but slightly to the west and inclined to the north. This is altogether far from the truth, for China should be in the center of the world, which we can prove by the single fact that we can see the North Star resting at the zenith of the heaven at midnight. How can China be treated like a small unimportant country, and placed slightly to the north as in this map?[7]

Given this view of the world, it is little wonder then that the Chinese, perhaps alone among the developed nations of the time, saw no need to send emissaries to other countries. Instead, for the Chinese, foreign relations consisted of tributary missions sent to the emperor from countries seeking trade with China. Any Chinese who left China to explore trade opportunities with "the outside" were thought to have abandoned their country.

The Qing took it for granted that they had the absolute right to "regulate foreigners trading with China, not only as to location and frequency, but down to the smallest details of personnel and goods involved."[8] Early in the Qing dynasty, when Dutch and Portuguese delegations tried to establish trade with China, they were forced to work with the Ministry of Rituals as "tributary nations" and were allowed to send trade missions only at approved intervals.

For the British, however, whose ships had begun to be seen off the east coast of China as early as 1635, these conditions and stipulations were unacceptable. To them, trade was what kept Britain's empire growing, and China was far too large a potential market to be allowed to remain closed off to the world economy. The next 200 years would see continuous British attempts to open China up to free trade.

The Rising British Empire

If China was a nation determined to remain uninterested in and isolated from the outside world, Great Britain was its polar opposite. Starting in 1497, when King Henry VIII commissioned John Cabot to find a route to Asia via the North Atlantic, British interests expanded ever outward until the empire's peak in about 1914, when it could truly be said that "the sun never sets on the British Empire."

As with most empires, progress and expansion came in fits and starts. After Cabot's voyage brought him not to Asia but to the coast of Newfoundland in North America, it would be nearly 100 years before England tried to extend its power beyond the British Isles. Internal strife, and intense competition with Spain, whose colonies in North, Central, and South America helped to make it the strongest Western nation of the time, stifled the possibility of acting on expansionist colonial ambitions.

By 1578, Great Britain felt secure enough within its own borders to begin exploration and colonization once again. The defeat of the Spanish Armada in 1588, along with the signing of a peace treaty with Spain in 1604, only served to speed up the process. Within a matter of years, Britain had established colonies throughout the Caribbean, as well as up and down the eastern seaboard of North America. These colonies served to provide the raw materials—spices, tobacco, and sugar, among others—that helped to power the British economy. At the same time the colonists living in those colonies provided a ready market for British products. It was, from the British point of view, an ideal economic situation.

In the 1770s, however, American colonists began to chafe against British rule. After a seven-year war of independence, the colonists defeated the British in 1783. The United States of America was born out of this conflict, and the loss of the American colonies hurt the British economically. So, too, did an economic and military struggle with France in the late eighteenth and early nineteenth centuries. Under Napoleon Bonaparte, who ruled France as first consul and later as emperor from 1799 to 1815, France threatened not only Britain's position on the world stage, but threatened to invade Britain itself. It was only after Napoleon's final defeat in 1815 that Great Britain was able to once again turn its attention to expanding, rather than merely defending, its empire.

EAST INDIA COMPANY

If England's initial impulse had been to go to Asia in search of colonies and trading partners, it was a dream that had long been pursued. Shortly after the defeat of the Spanish Armada in 1588 opened up the seas to British trade, a group of ambitious

(continues on page 32)

QUEEN VICTORIA

There are very few people whose names have become syn-
onymous with their time: Queen Victoria is one such person.
The Victorian age belongs to her.

She was born Alexandrina Victoria on May 24, 1819, the
daughter of Prince Edward Augustus Duke of Kent and Princess
Victoria of Saxe-Coburg-Saalfeld. A granddaughter of George
III and the niece of her predecessor on the throne, William
IV, the young princess Victoria became heiress presumptive
when William produced no surviving legitimate children. Upon
William's death on June 20, 1837, the 18-year-old Victoria
became queen of England. Her coronation took place one
year later, on June 28, 1838, and Victoria became the first
British monarch to take up residence at Buckingham Palace.

Two years later, Victoria married her first cousin, Prince
Albert of Saxe-Coburg and Gotha. (Since she was the monarch, she had to propose marriage to him.) The couple had
nine children before Prince Albert's death from typhoid fever
on December 14, 1861. His death devastated Victoria, who
was still recovering from the death of her mother earlier that
year. Victoria entered a state of mourning and wore black for
the rest of her life, rarely making public appearances and living in seclusion for most of the remainder of her days.

Despite this, her influence was enormous. Her reign as
queen lasted for 63 years and 7 months, longer than that
of any other British monarch to date. Her reign has since
become known as the Victorian era, a time of great industrial, political, and military progress within the United
Kingdom, but also of rigid sexual morality and manners.
Although Victoria became queen at a time when the United
Kingdom was already an established constitutional monarchy
in which the king or queen had very little political power,
her personal influence as a symbol of English strength and

The most influential figure of her era, Queen Victoria (1819-1901) is depicted here in her robes of state. At 63 years and 7 months, her reign lasted longer than that of any other British monarch.

morality was wide-ranging. The Victorian era represented the very height of the Industrial Revolution and saw a great expansion of the British Empire, a time in which it became the foremost global power.

(continued from page 29)
London merchants petitioned Queen Elizabeth for permission to sail to the Indian Ocean.

Permission granted, three ships left England in 1591, sailed around the Cape of Good Hope, on to the Arabian Sea; one of them, the *Edward Bonaventure*, then sailed on around Cape Comorin into the Malay Peninsula, finally returning to England in 1594. In 1596, three more ships sailed for the east; however, they were all lost at sea.

Just three years later, on September 24, 1599, another group of London merchants, having raised a considerable amount of capital, met to form a corporation, and set to work seeking Queen Elizabeth's approval. On December 31, 1600, the queen granted a Royal Charter to "George, Earl of Cumberland, and 215 Knights, Aldermen, and Burgesses" under the name "Governor and Company of Merchants trading into the East India," best known today as the British East India Company.[1]

The newly formed company was granted a monopoly of trade in the East Indies, meaning that it was the *only* British company allowed to do business with any of the islands of the East Indies—the vast string of islands in the Malay Peninsula between Asia and Australia. The only formal restriction placed on the company? It was not allowed to contest the earlier trading rights of "any Christian prince." While the company was a company like any other, with a governor and director and stockholders, it was also, in some ways, quite different. Few companies come complete with their own military, ready to use force if necessary to protect its interests.

The company had problems early in its existence, finding it difficult to establish a foothold in the spice trade against the already well-established Dutch. It did manage to open a factory in Bantam on the island of Java in Indonesia; imports of pepper from Java were an important part of the company's business for 20 years. As part of its business in Java, the company began docking ships at Surat, in India, which became a major trade transit point in 1608. Just two years later, it built its first factory in the town of Machilipatnam in the Indian state of Bengal, the first of many to come.

BATTLES AND EXPANSION

During this period of expansion, English traders often found themselves engaged in military action with their Dutch and Portuguese counterparts, who were also eager to establish themselves around the Indian Ocean. Although the British East India Company won a major victory over the Portuguese in the Battle of Swally in 1612, realizing the high cost of waging trade wars in distant seas, it decided to explore the possibility of gaining a larger foothold in mainland India. In 1615, Mughal Emperor Nuruddin Salim Jahangir granted the company exclusive rights to reside and build factories in Surat and other areas. It would be the first of many times that such rights were granted—or, in this case, basically given away.

What did the emperor get in return from the British? The company promised to provide the emperor with European goods and products. Jahangir thanked them by saying in a letter to King James:

> For confirmation of our love and friendship, I desire your Majesty to command your merchants to bring in their ships of all sorts of rarities and rich goods fit for my palace; and that you be pleased to send me your royal letters by every opportunity, that I may rejoice in your health and prosperous affairs; that our friendship may be interchanged and eternal.[2]

With the defeat of the Portuguese, the British were able to further expand their holdings in India, establishing bases in Goa, Chittagong, Madras, and Calcutta. By 1643, the company had 23 factories throughout India. Instead of spices from Malay, the company's business now consisted of cotton, silk, indigo dye, saltpeter, and tea. Then, after a rival English company attempted to challenge the company's monopoly in the late seventeenth century, the two companies were merged in 1708 to form what was formally known as the United Company of Merchants of England Trading to the East Indies, or, as it was more commonly known, the Honourable East India Company.

With a large part of India firmly under its control, the company began to search for new areas of economic expansion. China was the next obvious target. The company, however, along with the British government itself, began to chafe under Emperor Qianlong's restrictive trade policies—the British were allowed to trade only in the Chinese cities of Chou-shan (Zhoushan), Amoy (Xiamen), and Canton.

Canton, then as now, was the major port city of southern China. By restricting trade to Canton, however, the Chinese were able to keep the British (as well as other traders) at a distance from mainland China, since the city was a three-month trip overland to Peking, which is in a province separated by mountains from the rest of China. Control of trade was given to the viceroy of Kwangtung (Guangdong) and Kwangsi (Guangxi), a man appointed by the emperor to rule over an area larger than that of Britain. He, however, was not the person that the British traders would have to work with.

Instead, in 1720, Chinese merchants in Canton formed their own monopoly, a guild called the Cohong (from *gong-hong*, meaning "combined merchant companies"). In 1754, these merchants, commonly called "Hong," were each ordered by the Qing leadership to guarantee the good behavior and payment of dues of the foreign traders. These would be the people the British would work with, in a system guaranteed to keep contact between the barbarians and the Chinese government at a minimum. In those days, merchants were far down the ladder of social respectability in China, below scholars, craftsmen, and even farmers, so letting them deal with the foreigners seemed appropriate.

A view of the harbor at Canton showing the Hongs, circa 1767, when the British first sought to begin trading in China. Canton has been a major port of southern China for centuries.

Westerners could communicate only with the Hong. In turn, the Hong could only forward petitions and complaints from the foreigners to the Hoppo, a trade official appointed by the Qing. (The word *Hoppo* is not a Chinese word, but was derived from the Western pronunciation of a Chinese word;

in this case, it was the word for Qing government personnel.)
It was up to the Hoppo to decide whether foreigners' requests
would be forwarded to either the provincial governor or to
the emperor in Peking. He could, if he so chose, refuse to forward the documents at all, leaving the British unable to speak
directly with the only power in China that really mattered: the
emperor and his court.

It comes as no surprise that the British soon began to push
back against Qianlong's trade restrictions. By 1741, as historian Jonathan D. Spence points out, the British had learned
the importance of having a base in the Far East. (The Spanish
already had a base in Manila in the Philippines, the Dutch in
Batavia, now known as Jakarta, Indonesia.) In that year, George
Anson, a commodore in the Royal Navy who had orders to
attack Spanish shipping in the East, was forced to sail into
Canton harbor after his flagship suffered severe damage during
a storm. Anton believed that the Chinese, in accordance with
the international laws of the sea that were by then common in
the West, would treat him kindly as a neutral party in need of
assistance. He was wrong.

The multileveled bureaucracy in Canton threw as many
administrative barriers in his way as was humanly possible.
They refused to meet with him, or even to acknowledge his
messages to them, for many weeks. They overcharged him for
the poor quality supplies that they allowed him to purchase,
and even went so far as to refuse to allow him to make all
the repairs on his ship that he wanted. When Anson finally
returned to the West, his written account of his treatment in
China made headlines, and it helped to raise the level of anti-
Chinese feeling in Britain and throughout the West.

The East India Company tried again in 1759, sending James
Flint, a trader who had learned Chinese, to meet with the Qing
court and discuss British concerns regarding the restrictions
on trade in Canton as well as the rapidly growing corruption

among the Cohong. Bribes were often required to get approval for British goods being allowed into China.

Flint, sailing on a small ship named the *Success*, managed to reach the port city of Tientsin (today known as Tianjin) in northern China and have his complaints sent from there on to Peking. Initially, the emperor appeared open to talks, and sent a commission of investigation to Canton to study the matter. After the *Success* was lost at sea sailing back to Canton from Tientsin without Flint aboard, however, the emperor once again decided to take a firm stand against the foreigners. Flint was arrested and held in prison for three years on the charges of breaking Qing regulations against sailing to northern ports, for improperly presenting petitions, and even for having learned to speak Chinese.

The Qing followed up on the Flint incident by further tightening their restrictions against trade. After 1760, all foreign traders were restricted to using just the single port of Canton. On top of that, foreigners were not allowed to remain there except during the trading season, which lasted from October to March. Needless to say, moves such as this did little to ease the growing tensions between the traders of the Honourable East India Company and the Qing court, tensions that were only heightened by the failure of Lord Macartney's diplomatic mission of 1793.

Further complicating matters for the British was the growing imbalance of trade between the East India Company and China. The British were spending hundreds of thousands of pounds' worth of silver bars or ingots in exchange for Chinese silks, porcelain, and especially tea, all products that were popular back home.

The problem for the British was that although they were buying Chinese products (and slowly emptying out England's silver assets to do so), there was little that the Chinese wanted from the British. American traders, on the other hand, had some success in selling ginseng to Cantonese traders. They had even greater success selling seal pelts; a business that was so successful that within a single generation seals became almost extinct as the Americans over-killed the seals, destroying their breeding grounds.

The situation could not continue, or Britain would soon go broke purchasing Chinese tea. Between 1710 and 1759, the British paid £26,883,614 in gold and silver for tea, and selling only £9,248,306 worth of goods. In order to correct this imbalance of trade, a product would have to be found that the Chinese would want from the British as badly as the British wanted Chinese tea. Fortunately for the British, the success of the Honourable East India Company's takeover of India provided them with just such a product. Although its consumption there was illegal, it was Britain's last and best hope for making money in China.

Opium for Tea

The product was opium. Two questions, then, immediately arise: What exactly is opium and why did the Chinese want it so badly? The *Shorter Oxford English Dictionary* defines opium in this way: "A reddish-brown strong-scented addictive drug prepared from the thickened dried juice of the unripe capsules of the opium poppy, used (formerly esp. in the East) as a stimulant and intoxicant, and in medicine as a sedative and analgesic."[1]

In other words, the drug is a narcotic, one that relieves pain and causes pleasure. The drug, however, is also highly addictive. Once a user gets a taste for opium, his or her body requires the drug constantly. Jack Beeching describes the process in his book *The Chinese Opium Wars*:

A few grains of opium give the novice a feeling of eupho-
ria. His first pipe is the future addict's honeymoon; but
afterwards comes a wearisome listlessness. To face life once
more he must decide either to leave opium alone, or to go
on repeating and, usually, increasing his dose. The Chinese
formed from experience the view that one pipe smoked
daily for a week or ten days would leave a man in the grip of
addiction thereafter.

He would soon work up to three pipes a day . . . [and] a
three-pipe addict, denied his drug for longer than one day,
might expect to go through hell: a chill over the whole body,
an ache in all his limbs to the very bone, diarrhea, and ago-
nizing psychic misery. To break the habit by an act of will
was somewhat rare.[2]

The drug then, like most drugs, caused the user to pay a
nearly intolerable price for the pleasure that it brought. Lives,
families, and whole communities were shattered by opium use.
In this way, opium use in China is perhaps comparable to the
crack cocaine epidemic in the United States in the 1980s. The
user, desperate for his next fix, will undertake any means necessary, including crime, to obtain the money necessary to buy the
drug that his body is screaming out for.

Of course, opium has its proper medical uses as well,
including numbing pain. Indeed, records show that opium had
been used in China since the eleventh century as a painkiller
and as treatment for dysentery. The very name then used for
opium in China, *a-fu-jung*, derived from the Arabic, meant
"foreign medicine," and initially it was imported only in small
amounts to be used as a medicine, swallowed raw. Opium had
traveled to China from the Middle East along Arab trade routes
through Persia (now Iran), before arriving in India, and later,
China itself.

It was not until the seventeenth century—when knowledge
of opium-smoking techniques reached China—that opium

Although opium is a highly dangerous and addictive drug, it was used for medicinal purposes for many years. Seen here, a ceramic pharmaceutical jar for storing raw opium from 1632.

addiction began to slowly spread through the Chinese population, even before the British started bringing it in great quantities. (Smoking opium may have become popular because of the popularity of smoking tobacco, which had recently arrived from Latin America and had spread quickly through China.) Emperor Yongzheng soon learned of the growing problem and decided to ban opium in order to stop the problem before it became worse.

OPIUM USE IN ENGLAND

While the bulk of the opium controlled by the Honourable East India Company was sold in China, the company did sell opium to other countries, including its home country, Great Britain.

As in China, the first British opium addicts had been given the drug as a prescribed medicine, either in its raw medicinal form or as an alcoholic preparation of opium known as laudanum. Since at that time there was very little understanding of drug addiction, many doctors prescribed opium for nearly anything that ailed anybody. Indeed, Dr. John Brown of Edinburgh, a leading doctor of the time, taught that disease occurred because of either a lack or excess of excitement, and that laudanum was one of the best ways available to regain the body's proper balance of excitability.

Writers such as Samuel Coleridge and Thomas De Quincey became addicts. Coleridge himself, the author of such classic poems as "The Rime of the Ancient Mariner" and "Kubla Khan," was taking more than half a gallon of laudanum a week. William Wilberforce, the politician, philanthropist, and leader of the movement to halt the slave trade, was an opium addict for 45 years; he had first been given it as treatment for the medical condition known as gout.

Opium dealers were to be sentenced to wearing a heavy wooden collar known as the "cangue" for one month, after which they were to be banished to live in a distant military garrison, far away from large numbers of people. Individuals who helped entice people into opium dens—places where users could buy opium and then smoke it—were to be strangled. Individuals who either smoked or grew opium were to be beaten with 100 strokes. The Chinese believed that the heaviest

As in China, the use of opium quickly spread from the elite to the masses. For those who worked long hours in the factories of the British Industrial Revolution while living under appalling conditions, opium promised relief from their misery at a lower price than either beer or gin, earning it the nickname "Elevation." Even children found themselves taking opium, as their parents dosed them with patent medicines such as Godfrey's Cordial and Mother Bailey's Quieting Syrop, each of which contained large amounts of the narcotic.

Britain was not alone among Western nations in its use of opium. In the United States, President William Henry Harrison was treated with opium. During the U.S. Civil War, the Union Army used 2.8 million ounces (79.3 million grams) of opium tincture and more than 500,000 opium pills in treating wounded soldiers. Women, too, found themselves addicted to the narcotic, as doctors prescribed many medicines for "female problems" (largely due to painful menstruation) containing opium. It has been estimated that between 150,000 and 200,000 opium addicts lived in the United States during the late nineteenth century, with two-thirds of them women. It would not be until the early twentieth century that opium use began to decline, once laws were put in place and new drugs replaced it as a painkiller.

punishment should fall on those who sold opium or encouraged others to smoke it, not on those who used it.

The question remains though: Why did the Chinese of this period fall so easily into the trap of opium addiction? Spence points out that while there is no Chinese literature of the time that discusses this, it is possible to speculate on the reasons.

Chinese documents of the period do indicate that, at least initially, opium became popular among groups that normally faced either boredom or stress in their lives. Thus, eunuchs of the court smoked opium, as did Manchu court officials, who often had tedious bureaucratic jobs. Women in well-to-do households, unable to get an education or even to leave the walled compounds of their palatial homes, smoked opium to help ease the boredom. Secretaries (always male) in magistrate's offices smoked it. Merchants putting together business deals, students preparing for the rigorous state examinations—even soldiers on their way to battle against rebels against the emperor smoked it.

THE BRITISH STEP IN

Initially, it was Dutch and French traders who began bringing small amounts of opium into China. The British, despite having inherited the Indian Moghul emperor's monopoly on high-quality Patna opium when they conquered the Indian state of Bengal, were hesitant to sell the product. In fact, in 1771, the East India Company's Select Committee at Canton asked the presidents of Madras and Bombay to stop all opium exports from India to China. Since opium was technically illegal throughout China itself, bringing it into the country made legal trade difficult. This reluctance, however, soon faded when confronted with economic realities.

For decades, the British had paid for Chinese tea with Spanish silver, the currency that the Chinese trusted the most. When Spain became an ally of the United States in its war of revolution against Great Britain, however, the British found themselves unable to buy Spanish silver. By 1781, no Spanish silver had reached India for two years. At the same time, two years worth of opium production was sitting in warehouses, unsold. The solution to the British problem was painfully obvious. Historian Jack Beeching observed:

> Into [British] hands had accidentally fallen abundant supplies of a product which any keen merchant might be forgiven for regarding as the answer to his dream—an article which sold itself, since any purchaser who has acquired a taste for opium always comes back anxiously for more, cash in hand.[3]

Wasting no time, the East India Company bowed to the inevitable and established a monopoly for the purchase of Indian opium. It then sold licenses to Western merchants known as "country traders" for the right to participate in the opium trade. In this way, the East India Company was not directly selling the opium to the Chinese; it was done indirectly, while still allowing the company to profit from the illegal trade.

When the country traders sold their opium in China, they deposited the silver that they received in payment with company agents in Canton in exchange for letters of credit. The company, in turn, was able to use the silver to buy porcelain, silk, and most importantly, tea, for sale in Britain. This established a "triangle of trade," moving goods from Britain to India, India to China, and then China to Britain; enabling every British trader concerned to make a profit at each step.

FIRST SHIPMENT

It would take time for opium addiction to spread, because the initial British shipments of opium to China did not go well. In 1781, Governor William Hastings of Bengal sent two ships to China loaded with 3,450 chests of opium, each chest containing between 130 and 160 pounds (59 and 72.5 kilograms) of

Once opium use became widespread in China, addicts sought places where they could smoke it at their leisure. Here, Chinese opium smokers are photographed in an opium den, circa 1880.

opium. One of these ships, the armed sloop *Betsy*, was captured by a French privateer, the *St. Therese*. (A privateer is a privately owned warship commissioned to attack and raid the merchant ships of an enemy nation. They are, in essence, pirate ships.) The second ship, *Nonsuch*, flying under the false colors of France and Spain, managed to avoid the pirates and reached the Portuguese-controlled island of Macao in July 1782.

Initially, there were no buyers for the illegal cargo, since the official Hong merchants still disapproved of purchasing contraband materials. One Hong merchant called Sinqua made an offer of $210 a chest, but since the captain of the *Nonsuch* had paid $500 a chest for the opium, he refused the offer. Even so, he ended up selling what he could of his entire cargo at the bargain price of just $840. Governor Hastings's initial attempt at selling opium lost him nearly a quarter of a million dollars.

It would be one of the few times that an attempt to sell opium in China lost money. Spence points out, "For opium to sell steadily in China, several factors were necessary: the narcotic had to be available in large quantities; there had to be a developed means of consuming it; enough people had to want to smoke it to make the trade viable, and government attempts at prohibition had to be ineffectual."[4]

The British had growing amounts of opium to sell. The Chinese had the knowledge necessary to turn raw medicinal opium into an easily abused substance, ready to smoke. A growing number of people, bored and dissatisfied with the slowly declining Qing dynasty, were ready to turn to drugs in an effort to make their lives at least seem more bearable.

The one question remaining was whether the Chinese would be able to stop the British from bringing opium into the country. It would take several decades and two wars to settle that question once and for all.

5

First Moves

Noting that opium smoking was spreading from the coastal areas in to the nation's interior, the Chinese emperor laid down even stricter penalties in 1799 to fight it. The edict banned opium smoking as well as its importation into the country. Indeed, opium was the only item to be excluded from the trading that was allowed by foreigners at Canton. "Foreigners obviously derive the most solid profits and advantages," said the emperor's decree, "but that our countrymen should pursue this destructive and ensnaring vice . . . is indeed odious and deplorable."[1]

For the Honourable East India Company, this edict should have posed a serious legal and moral problem. How could the company justify selling opium to a nation where the use of opium was illegal? Unfortunately for all concerned, economics were of paramount importance. The company relied on its business in tea to remain profitable. The British government depended on its tax on tea to provide a large part of its revenue. Opium was the only thing the British had to offer that the Chinese were willing to pay money for. In 1799, the same year as the imperial edict tightened the ban on opium, nearly 4,000 chests, or 20 times the amount that was needed for strictly medicinal purposes, had been brought into the country.

Since the East India Company was not actually carrying the opium itself, its directors tried to convince themselves that the company played no part in its sale in China. The opium that did arrive in China, however, brought by the country traders who purchased it directly from the East India Company at auction.

At this time, it was still company policy to limit production as much as possible in order to increase demand and therefore raise the price. Chests of opium containing 40 balls of opium per chest (each about the size of a tennis ball), encased in a shell of dried poppy shells, were sold at auction in Calcutta at prices that reached four times the actual costs of production. The money earned by the company from the opium trade doubled between 1773 and 1783; by 1793, the monies earned went very far in remedying the trade imbalance between Great Britain and China.

HOW DID THE TRADE WORK?

As previously mentioned, all of China's foreign trade (with the exception of a Russian caravan in the north along the Gobi Desert) was done just outside the city of Canton. It took place in a series of grim offices and warehouses that were between the river and the 25-foot-high (7.6-meter-high) walls surrounding the city, a place that became known as the Factory.

It was in the Factory that the foreign merchants resided from November until March, the only time they were allowed to remain there. In this five-month period, China's annual tea crop arrived by boat from inland, and eager traders ready to make deals bargained for prices. Foreigners, however, were not allowed to enter the city of Canton itself. Not only that, foreigners were not permitted to carry weapons, and women were left waiting on the island of Macao, where the traders spent their time between the months of April and October.

This was where and how legitimate trade occurred. After the emperor's 1799 edict, however, most Cohong merchants were unwilling to deal directly and openly for opium, so a more discrete means of trade was found. Foreign traders quickly discovered that if they anchored their ships loaded with opium at selected spots along the coast, Chinese traders would easily be able to make their way out to them to purchase their opium stocks. Large fortified ships anchored off Lintin Island in the bay below Canton became a convenient point of distribution for opium. There, Chinese traders, either sailing or rowing, could stay clear of any attempts by the nearly nonexistent Qing Navy to capture them. After getting the opium back to land, these adventurers were able to distribute the opium by road and river, deeper and deeper into mainland China.

For the next 20 years, the amount of opium illegally brought into China remained fairly steady, rarely rising above 5,000 chests per year. This was because of the fact that the East India Company still wanted to keep production low in order to help keep prices high. Because prices were still high, the only people who could afford opium were members of the elite. For the vast majority of Chinese, opium remained a luxury item that they were unable to afford or even contemplate purchasing. This, however, would soon change.

A CHANGE OF STRATEGY

Several factors came into play around 1820 that changed the rules of the game for opium trade in China. One of these, oddly enough, involved the increased use of steam power in textile manufacturing. In 1817, the East India Company, by an act of Parliament, had lost its monopoly of trade to India, although it did maintain its control of trade between Britain and China. Why the change? Because textile manufacturers in Britain, due to steam power, were able to produce cloth so cheaply and of such high quality that they were able to flood India with their products, earning vast amounts of money for themselves—while putting large numbers of traditional Indian loom workers out of business in the process.

Who in India was able to purchase the British-made cloth? It was the opium growers of Bengal themselves, who, having been paid in cash by the government for their crop, were able to afford cloth from Britain. The more opium being grown in India meant that more cotton cloth was being purchased, which meant greater earnings for the British government. Yet the East India Company's policy was still to limit opium production, which placed it in direct opposition to the wishes of both the British cotton mills and the British government. Then another factor came into play that tipped the balance in favor of greater opium production at lower prices.

Somewhat to the surprise of the British, it turned out that opium could be and was grown in places outside of Bengal. Because the East India Company had, in effect, washed its hands of direct involvement in the opium trade (once it had auctioned off the opium itself), it was helpless to act when American and Portuguese traders began selling Turkish opium, a decidedly inferior product, at prices far below British prices. Additionally, an independent source of Indian opium, known as Malwa opium, grown in the nortwest region of Rajputana, was being sold at prices far below that of the Patna opium that was controlled by the East India Company in Bengal. (In 1818, however, that independent source of opium fell under British control as well.)

As Jack Beeching makes clear in his book *The Chinese Opium Wars*, the British government was determined to ensure that there was a continuous flow of tea from Canton, since 10 percent of its revenue was now coming from its tea tax. As

Beeching points out, however, that tea was bought by silver earned from the sale of opium, and it was the opium growers in India who were the fastest growing market for English cottons manufactured in Lancashire.

WESTERNERS AND THE CHINESE LEGAL SYSTEM

During the later years of Emperor Qianlong's reign, there were a number of legal cases involving Westerners that raised concern among the British traders, who found themselves faced with a legal system that they did not understand or respect.

In one case in 1773, Portuguese authorities in Macao tried an Englishman who was accused of killing a Chinese man. They found him innocent and released him. Qing officials, however, insisted that they had the right to prosecute homicide cases in which the victim was Chinese. They retried the Englishman themselves and had him executed. Seven years later, Qing officials went even further, asserting their right to intervene even in cases where one foreigner killed another foreigner on Chinese soil. A Frenchman who had killed a Portuguese sailor in a fight was forced out of the French consul, where he had taken refuge, and was publicly executed by strangulation.

The two cases that most angered the Westerners into reconsidering how to deal with the Qing, however, both involved trading vessels: the *Lady Hughes* and the *Emily*. In 1784, nine years before Macartney's visit to China, the *Lady Hughes*, under license to the British East India Company and trading between China and India, fired a salute near Canton, the discharge of which killed two Chinese bystanders.

The Honourable East India Company was no longer able to resist the combined political and economic pressure. The company decided it would both lower its prices and increase its production—aided, in part, by its new control of the source of

---

When the ship's captain told the Chinese that he could not prove which gunner had actually fired the shot, the Chinese, who believed in the concept of *baojia*—the idea that all members of a community are responsible for the acts of that community—arrested the ship's business manager. They also threatened to stop all trade with the West until the person responsible was turned over to them. After a tense standoff, the *Lady Hughes* turned the gunner who was probably responsible for the crime over to the Chinese. He was strangled in January 1785.

In the case of the United States merchant ship *Emily*, a crewman on the ship accidentally dropped an earthenware pitcher onto the head of a Chinese fruit seller on a boat below, who fell overboard and drowned. The Chinese insisted that the crewman, named Terranova, be turned over to them, but the Americans insisted they would hold the trial themselves aboard ship. However, after the Qing ordered the halt of all American trade in Canton (and, perhaps, because the hold of the *Emily* was filled with illegal opium), the ship's captain gave in, and Terranova was turned over to Chinese authorities. After a trial that no Westerners were allowed to attend, he was found guilty and executed the next day.

It was cases such as these that convinced Western traders that the Chinese must be forced to give up their right to arrest and try foreigners, which gave Great Britain just one more excuse to do whatever it felt necessary to compel China to give in to British demands.

Malwa opium. While previously the company had been reluctant to be involved in the opium trade, that policy changed abruptly after 1819. The new policy was "to endeavor to secure the command of the Market by furnishing a Supply [of opium] on so enlarged a scale . . . as shall prevent competition."[2]

The company quickly beat back its competition in opium sales to China by underselling the Americans and cutting off the Portuguese access to their source of supply in Turkey. This left the company with a new problem: how to sell its new, greatly increased stocks of opium. As Beeching noted, "In other words: so that the British public could go on drinking their millions of gallons of tea each year, twice as many Chinese opium addicts . . . had somehow to be created."[3]

China itself seemed paralyzed by inaction: What could the Chinese government do to stop the flow of opium? Emperor Daoguang, who reigned from 1821 to 1850, was, in the words of Jonathan D. Spence, "a well-meaning but ineffective man"[4] who, while concerned about the spread of opium addiction, remained uncertain just how to solve the problem.

The problem for China went beyond that of just opium addiction; it was one of economics as well. By 1825, it became clear to Daoguang that so much Chinese silver was flowing out of the country to pay for the opium that the national economy was becoming damaged. Less silver available meant that the price of silver rose in relation to copper. Copper currency was what peasants used in daily life, but taxes had to be paid in silver, which was rapidly becoming more expensive. This put additional pressure on a peasant population that was already struggling to make a living, and the emperor and his court saw an unhappy peasantry as a threat to himself and his dynasty.

The amount of silver moving out of China and into British coffers continued to increase, as did the amount of opium flowing into China. Between 1829 and 1840, approximately $7 million entered China; at the same time $56 million had been "sucked out."[5] This kind of financial pressure was just one more way for the British to force the Chinese to do their bidding and open their nation up to trade. As the newspaper the *Chinese Courier* pointed out in 1833, "perhaps nothing could contribute more readily to the final reduction of the Chinese to reasonable terms with foreigners than this steady, non-ceasing impoverishment of the country."[6]

The British, though, were determined both to continue selling opium and to open up a full trade and diplomatic relationship with China. With the end of the East India Company's monopoly in 1834, the British government appointed 48-year-old Lord Napier of Meristoun as chief superintendent of trade in China. A naval officer with no experience as a businessman, he was sent by the British Crown as its representative in the hope that he would be able to receive the recognition from the emperor that two previous British ambassadors had failed to achieve.

THE NAPIER FIZZLE

Lord Napier's mission was probably doomed from the start, due in no small part to his physical appearance. He was tall, lean, and bony, with a head of red hair—a look that matched up exactly with the Chinese stereotype of the Red Barbarian. To the Chinese, he was, physically at least, laughable.

Foreign Secretary Henry John Temple, Third Viscount Palmerston, more commonly known as Lord Palmerston, sent Napier on his mission with very specific instructions— instructions that often enough came up against Chinese law. Although told to obey Chinese regulations, Napier was ordered to set up base in the city of Canton itself. Technically Canton was off-limits to him: the Factory was to be used only by merchants, and then only while tea was being shipped. Napier was not only not a merchant, but he was to arrive in midsummer, long after tea season had ended.

Next, Napier was ordered to communicate directly with Chinese authorities, something that was next to impossible, as all contact between foreign merchants and Chinese authorities took place through the Cohong. A threat of force might lead to direct talks with Chinese authorities, but Napier, while pressured to bring about such talks, was also instructed to "cautiously abstain from making any appeal for the protection of our military and naval forces."[7]

Napier's principal assignment was, as his title indicated, to superintend trade. His superiors told him that he was not to interfere in any way with the ongoing coastal trade in opium, no matter how much that trade angered the Chinese: "It is not desirable that you should encourage such adventures, but you must never lose sight of the fact that you have no authority to interfere with them or prevent them."[8] In addition, he was instructed to survey the Chinese coastline (and of course, the only British seamen who could assist him with this were the opium traders themselves) and to begin the process of selecting sites the British Navy could use, just in case war became necessary.

There was, of course, no way for Lord Napier to fulfill his instructions without angering the very Chinese authorities he had been sent to negotiate with. His mission got off to a bad start when he arrived in Macao, along with his wife and two unmarried daughters, on July 15, 1834. Napier immediately sent a letter to Lu K'un, the viceroy at Canton, announcing his arrival. The viceroy, of course, was not permitted to take official notice of Napier's arrival himself—such word had to come from the Cohong.

A week later, the viceroy issued an edict, stating that "the . . . Barbarian Eye, if he wishes to come to Canton, must inform the Hong merchants, so that they may petition me."[9] Although aware of Chinese regulations, Napier decided to ignore the viceroy's edict and instead sailed on his ship, the frigate *Andromache*, to the mouth of the Pearl River. He left at the same time that the Hong merchants who were trying to stop him were en route to Macao.

This 1882 English illustration depicts the sale of opium in China. Despite the emperor's best efforts at a crackdown, the opium trade flourished in China and addicted millions of Chinese.

It should be noted that not every British trader was in favor of employing such aggressive efforts against China; moreover, not every British trader was selling opium or in favor of selling opium. Legitimate tea traders were willing to wait for China's trade policy to change on its own, and many disliked the opium dealers for fear that Chinese reaction against them would harm their legal and legitimate tea trade.

Lord Napier transferred from the *Andromache* to the frigate's cutter under the watchful eyes of the Chinese at their forts at the Bogue and was rowed 40 miles (64.3 km) upstream to the English Factory located under the city wall. In response,

(continues on page 60)

WILLIAM JARDINE

It perhaps may be considered ironic that William Jardine (February 24, 1784–February 27, 1843) began his career as a ship's surgeon before becoming the most successful opium trader of his day and the driving force behind the First Opium War.

Jardine was born on a small farm near Lochmaben, Dumfriesshire, Scotland. Although his family struggled to make ends meet, his older brother, David, helped to provide him with the means to go to school and start a career. In 1800, Jardine entered the University of Edinburgh, where he took classes in anatomy, medical practice, and obstetrics, while being apprenticed to a surgeon who provided him with housing, food, and experience working in hospitals. After graduating from the Royal College of Surgeons of Edinburgh, Jardine entered the service of the British East India Company in 1802 at the age of 18.

Although he had signed on as a surgeon's mate in the East India Company's Maritime Marine Service onboard the *Marchantman Brunswick,* he quickly learned that there were even easier ways available to him to make money. One benefit of being in the service of the East India Company was that employees were able to trade in goods for their own profit. Each employee was allowed cargo space equivalent to two chests, or approximately 100 pounds (45.3 kg) of cargo. Jardine soon realized that he had a natural aptitude for trade, and even leased the cargo space of other crewmen who were uninterested in using it themselves.

Jardine soon saved enough money to become an independent trader. In 1817, he left the East India Company to go into partnership with two others traders, Thomas Weeding and Framjee Cowasjee. The firm did very well in the domain of private traders, and 11 years later, Jardine was in business with another prominent trader, William Matheson, as part of the leading firm Magniac & Company.

There, Jardine developed a reputation as being a tough, serious, detail-oriented worker, who worked well with the more creative, outspoken, and jovial Matheson. Despite their differences in personality, both men were hardworking and single-minded in their pursuit of wealth. By 1832, the two men joined forces in forming a new agency: Jardine, Matheson & Company.

When, one year later, the British Parliament ended the East India Company's monopoly of trade between Britain and China, Jardine, Matheson & Company was poised to fill the void. With its first voyage carrying tea, the Jardine clipper ship *Sarah* left China for Britain, and Jardine, Matheson & Company was transformed from a major commercial agent of the East India Company into the largest British trading Hong, or firm, in Asia. William Jardine was now referred to by other traders as "Tai-pan," a Chinese colloquial term meaning "Great Manager."

By 1841, Jardine's company had 19 intercontinental clipper ships, as well as hundreds of small ships and crafts used for coastal and upriver smuggling. The trading concerns included smuggling opium into China from India, trading spices and sugar from the Philippines, importing Chinese tea and silk into England, handling cargo papers and insurance, renting dockyard facilities and warehouse space, trade financing, and other aspects of business and trade.

When Commissioner Lin Zexu began his crackdown on the illegal Chinese opium trade, it was William Jardine who went to London in 1838 to urge Lord Palmerston to go to war with China. Palmerston decided mainly based on the advice of Jardine and his report, known as the Jardine Paper, to go

(continues)

(continued)

to war. After China's defeat and the subsequent signing of the Treaty of Nanking, the illegal opium trade grew, as did the firm of Jardine, Matheson & Company, which became known as the "Princely Hong" for being the largest British trading firm in East Asia.

William Jardine did not live to see his company's greatest successes. He died on February 27, 1843, as one of the richest and most powerful men in Britain, as well as a respected member of Parliament. The company that he began, now known as the Jardine Matheson Group, is still active in Hong Kong, where it remains one of the largest conglomerates there and its largest private employer, second only to the government.

(continued from page 57)

Chinese customs agents had already gone through Lord Napier's trunks, and Chinese boatmen were being taken out of his service, both signals that the Chinese were not at all happy with Napier's decision to go to Canton. This, however, was just the beginning.

Although Napier had been instructed to contact Lu K'un directly, no procedures existed that would allow that to take place. There was only one option. At the perimeter of the foreign settlement was a gate that led into Canton. There, petitions could be, in theory at least, turned over to Chinese authorities. It was up to Napier's secretary, J.H. Astell, to try to get the petition through.

Armed with a letter to the viceroy and accompanied by a group of British merchants for support, Astell went to the Petition Gate. There was, however, a problem. Only documents that used the Chinese character *pin*, meaning "petition," could be officially accepted from foreigners. Because Astell's document was clearly a letter, not a petition, the mandarin on duty refused to take it. A mandarin of higher rank, however, was already on his way to the gate to look into the matter.

As hours passed, a crowd of Chinese gathered and began shouting at the Briton. When the higher-ranked mandarin arrived, he, too, refused to accept the letter. Finally, a group of Hong merchants arrived at the gate, bowed, and offered to take the document themselves. Astell, under orders only to give the letter to Chinese government officials, refused their offer. So the impasse continued.

Additional mandarins arrived. They, too, refused to accept the document. The British found themselves playing a game under Chinese rules that they did not really understand and under which they had no chance of winning. After three hours in the blazing sun, Astell retreated back to the Factory, while Lu K'un reported back to the emperor that "it is plain, on the least reflection, that in order to distinguish the Chinese from outsiders it is of the utmost importance to maintain dignity and sovereignty."[10] If the battle remained that of Napier vs. the rigid Chinese bureaucracy, there was no way that Napier could win.

Napier ran up against an additional roadblock when it became known that he had gone to Canton from Macao without receiving his red permit, the passport the Chinese required of all foreigners going to the Factories. The viceroy sent an edict to the Hong merchants—in which he transposed Lord Napier's name phonetically into two Chinese characters which signified "Laboriously Vile"—stating that when Napier had finished his business in Canton, he was to return immediately to Macao and wait there to receive his red permit. "Should the said Laboriously Vile oppose and disobey, it will be because the Hong merchants have mismanaged the affair. In that case I shall be obliged to report against them."[11] Days later, Lu K'un increased the pressure on Napier, withdrawing his permission to remain in Canton until Napier had completed his business and ordering him to return to Macao immediately.

Lord Napier decided to ignore the viceroy's order, backed in his decision by businessmen such as William Jardine, one of the most successful of the opium traders. Jardine hoped that such insults to the British king's representative by the Chinese would anger the British population and help to bring about armed British intervention in China. Napier, a retired naval officer, was easy to persuade. Under pressure from Jardine, Napier wrote Lord Palmerston, who was back in Britain, on August 14: "Three or four frigates and brigs, with a few steady British troops . . . would settle the thing."[12] The letter would then have to go by ship around the Cape of Good Hope before reaching Britain.

Owing to this same difficulty in communication, Napier was unaware that the British Cabinet that had appointed him was out of power by the time he had arrived in Canton. The new foreign secretary, the Duke of Wellington, detested Palmerston and the businessmen who were pressuring Britain to force China to open up its trade by any means necessary, including war. Wellington sent a dispatch to Napier on February 2, 1835, making clear that the government's policy toward China did not include the use of force to establish economic ties. Napier, however, did not live long enough to read his new instructions.

On August 16, in response to Napier's refusal to return to Macao, Viceroy Lu K'un ordered a partial stoppage of trade between China and all foreign traders. The next day, the *Andromache*, along with the frigate *Imogene*, returned to Canton. Napier, perhaps feeling more confident now that he had two British warships behind him, sent a dispatch to Lord Grey attacking the Chinese government, saying that its representatives were "in the extreme degree of mental imbecility and moral degradation, dreaming themselves to be the only people on earth, and being entirely ignorant of the theory and practice of international law."[13]

In this dispatch, Napier argued that the British should respond to the partial stoppage of trade by sending military and naval forces into the area, ready to attack by September of the following year. "What," Lord Napier asked, "can an army of bows and arrows and pikes and shields do against a handful of British veterans?"[14] Napier was confident that the emperor would sign a commercial treaty on terms favorable to the British once British troops arrived.

In this regard, Napier was right. As Beeching correctly points out, "Though the Chinese might go on haughtily treating the British as they always had done—as barbarians—they were, in the long run, the losing side."[15] At this point in China's history, there was no way that their military could stand up against the more advanced military of the British.

What Viceroy Lu K'un counted on, however, was the fact that the trade embargo would hit some merchants harder than others, and that support for Napier would suffer accordingly. Napier, in an attempt to go over the viceroy's head, put up a poster addressed to the citizens of Canton themselves, pointing out that the trade embargo hit them as well, and deploring the "ignorance and obstinacy"[16] of Lu K'un. Not unexpectedly, the viceroy struck back with words of his own:

> A lawless foreign slave has issued a notice. We do not know how such a barbarian dog can have the audacity to call himself an Eye (that is to say, an official). . . . Though a savage from beyond the pale, his sense of propriety would have restrained him from such an outrage. It is a capital offence to incite the people against their rulers, and we would be justified in obtaining a mandate for his decapitation.[17]

On September 2, Lu K'un issued an edict ordering all trade between China and Britain stopped. The British were ordered to leave Canton and return to either Whampoa or Macao. Their Chinese servants were taken away from them, their supplies cut off, and their Factories surrounded by armed Chinese troops. The next move was Lord Napier's.

Napier responded to the viceroy's edict by ordering the *Imogene* and the *Andromache* to move back up the river to Whampoa. If the forts protecting the estuary should fire on the *Imogene*, it was to fire back. The *Imogene* was further ordered to anchor at Whampoa—as high up the Pearl River as a frigate could go—and wait there to protect the Factories.

On September 7, the two ships entered the Bogue River and began moving toward the mouth of the Pearl. The Chinese fired at the ships, at first with blanks as a warning to turn back, then for real. The British quickly returned fire, easily knocking out the Chinese ability to attack. Continuing up the river, the British arrived at Whampoa and waited for the Chinese's next move.

Meanwhile, back in Canton, Lord Napier, upon learning that the Chinese had dared to attack his ships, once again expressed his anger toward the viceroy: "It is a very serious offence to fire on or otherwise insult the British flag. . . . They have opened the preliminaries of war."[18] For his part, Lu K'un responded that "if the said Barbarian Eye will speedily . . . withdraw his ships of war and remain obedient to the old rules . . . I will yet give some slight indulgence."[19]

Although the British military force was strong, the Chinese had the upper hand. They had Napier and his men surrounded in Canton, and the Chinese then blocked the two British ships from moving either farther up the river or back down. With neither side willing to withdraw from the standoff, the likelihood that war might break out seemed to many to be a real possibility.

Yet it did not happen. Lord Napier, who had suffered from an intermittent fever contracted in the hot and humid weather of Canton, became so ill that his doctor thought it best that he return to Macao for treatment. To maintain his dignity, it was proposed that he sail back to Macao aboard a British frigate. The Chinese, however, seeing victory in hand, refused to grant his request.

Seen here, workers open balls of opium in Indochina. After the raw opium was allowed to dry for several weeks, it was stored in clay pots. It was then weighed, tested, valued, thrown into large vats, kneaded, and pressed into spheres the size of small cannon balls.

After much negotiation between the British and the Hong merchants, the Chinese announced that if the British frigates retreated down the Pearl River to Lintin Island (which, by doing so, would indicate that the reason the British Navy had been there in the first place was to protect the opium trade), then Napier would be allowed to return to Macao. As a final insult, however, he would not be allowed to travel on a British ship. Instead, he would have to go on a Chinese ship, under an escort of Chinese military guards, just like a common criminal.

The 88-mile (141.6 km) trip took five days. Just days after finally arriving in Macao, Lord Napier died on October 11,

1834. His mission, which became known as the "Napier Fizzle," had been, from the British point of view, a complete and utter failure. It had also, however, revealed just how weak the long-term Chinese position was. If and when the British decided to use full military force against the Chinese, it was obvious that the Chinese would not stand a chance.

The fact that Chinese military technology lagged behind the British became even more evident on January 1, 1836. On that date, the *Jardine* made its way into the mouth of the Pearl River for her first trip to Canton, the first ship powered by steam to do so. The Chinese were impressed by the new technology, but at the same time immediately banned its use on the Pearl River. The machinery was removed from the ship, but the point had been made. As Beeching described it:

> Mount a gun in a small steamer, and for the first time in history you had a ship-of-war independent of wind and tide, able to beat against the monsoon, and to operate effectively up rivers and in shallow coastal waters. Against this technically advanced weapon of war, the Chinese in coming years would have no possible means of defense.[20]

If the Chinese, equipped with only sailing ships and antiquated guns, were not going to be able to defeat the British militarily, they would have to find other means to stop them from flooding their country with opium.

6

Commissioner Lin vs. the British

Emperor Daoguang and his imperial court once again began to consider their options regarding the opium trade. The evidence by that time was undeniable: China was being flooded with high-quality, low-cost opium, and the number of addicts was growing at an alarming rate. In 1836, one British doctor estimated that the amount of opium entering the country was enough to satisfy the needs of 12,500,000 smokers. Two years later, the viceroy of Hupeh and Hunan estimated that there were more than 4,000,000 opium addicts in China. Clearly, the free trade of opium was infecting China with a nearly insatiable addiction for the drug.

The government examined two options. It was argued by some that perhaps it would be better to simply legalize the opium trade. By doing so, it would end the corruption and blackmailing of officials and would bring in badly needed revenue through tariffs. (In 1836, the bribe necessary to get a chest of opium ashore in Canton rose from $30 to $60.) In addition, it was argued that it would be better to simply allow the Chinese to grow their own opium. By doing so, they would cut off the trade of Indian opium.

That, however, was a minority view. Most of the emperor's court felt not only that opium should continue to be outlawed but that the laws should be made even stricter and the punishments more severe. If not, they argued, the dynasty was doomed to fall. One of the emperor's advisers, Lin Zexu, bluntly described the potential results of allowing the opium trade to continue as it had, saying that "a few decades from now we shall not only be without soldiers to resist the enemy, but also in want of silver to provide an army."[1]

The Chinese began a new crackdown. It became more difficult for Chinese ships to make the run between the British opium ships docked at Lintin and the villages around the Bay of Canton. As the opium accumulated at Lintin and prices began to drop, the trade became more daring. Ships began bringing the opium farther up the coast and even up the Pearl River past the Bogue Forts to Whampoa. William Matheson, of the opium-trading firm Magniac & Company, wrote to a client, "We are doing everything in our power to work the article off on the coast and among the islands in European boats."[2]

The new superintendent of trade, Captain Charles Elliot, had little control over the free traders in opium. His primary job was to make sure that the tea crop was shipped safely out of China, tea that was paid for by the illegal opium trade. So even though he did not personally approve of the opium trade, he was not to interfere.

The Chinese, though, were determined to keep the pressure on the British traders. On December 12, 1838, a Chinese official arrived at the exercise yard outside of the Canton Factories and his men raised an execution cross, upon which an infamous

Daoguang (1782–1850), the emperor of China from 1820 to 1850, is depicted in an English lithograph, circa 1842. China's problems with opium use grew during his reign, despite his efforts to suppress it.

opium den owner, Ho Lao-chin, was to be strangled in front of the foreigner's faces, to show them the results of their crimes.

The chained, condemned man was brought in, given one last opium pipe to smoke (ironic, given his crime), and was about to be tied to the cross when a group of British sailors broke in, destroyed the cross, and began attacking the Chinese who had gathered to witness the execution. An even larger crowd of Chinese gathered to attack the British sailors, and a near riot took place. It was evident to all that tensions were quickly mounting between the British and the Chinese.

By the end of 1839, the Chinese anti-opium campaign had spread throughout China, and the British opium traders were clearly becoming concerned about the future of their profitable business. William Jardine became convinced that if the Chinese campaign should continue for another year, opium consumption within China would likely decline by two-thirds, as would his earnings.

Given the economic necessity for the opium trade, it seemed likely that the British could not and would not allow that to occur. The British and the Indian governments had become dependent on the revenue from the illegal opium trade. In truth, it was, as Elliot described it, the 300 or so opium traders who were the basis of a triangle of trade that kept the British economy—and in effect, the British government—afloat.

To the Chinese, it was impossible to even imagine that simple merchants could have that kind of power and influence over a government. In China, merchants were still considered social inferiors. By extension, as Jack Beeching points out, "That by suppressing the Canton opium trade their Imperial Commissioner would throw down a challenge to the entire British Empire would also have seemed extremely far-fetched."[3] The Chinese, however, were finally determined to wipe out the opium trade once and for all. To do so, they appointed Lin Zexu as imperial commissioner to end the opium trade on December 31, 1838.

COMMISSIONER LIN

The choice appeared to be a wise one. Lin, the former governor-general of Hubei and Hunan, had been a longtime opponent of opium smoking and opium smokers and was known for his high standards of morality. (His nickname was "Lin the Clear Sky.") Upon his arrival at Canton, he immediately set out to work. He initiated a series of public proclamations—similar to modern public service announcements—that served to educate the public about the health risks of opium consumption, while also ordering all smokers to turn over their pipes and opium to his staff within two months.

At the same time, education officials were made to discover whether any university degree-holders were opium users. If so, they would be punished; the others were organized into groups of five, with each pledging to guarantee that the others in the group would not smoke. In a clever ploy similar to traditional examinations, Lin summoned 600 students to a special assembly. There, in addition to questions about classic Chinese literature, they were asked to name, anonymously if they wanted, the major opium distributors and to come up with ways to suppress the opium trade. Similar tactics were used among military and naval personnel. The local gentry were asked to form a neighborhood watch system to discover addicts in their community. By the middle of 1839, more than 1,600 Chinese had been arrested, and more than 35,000 pounds (15,875 kg) of opium and 43,000 opium pipes had been seized or turned in.

Lin knew that while it was important for him to stomp out opium use among the Chinese, it was just as important for him to stop the British from bringing opium into the country in the first place. He began by taking steps against the Cohong merchants, lecturing them for posting bonds stating that certain British merchants, such as William Jardine and James Innes, were not opium traders, when it was obvious that they were.

Lin then took two major steps that started him on a collision course with the British. First, he ordered that foreign opium dealers were subject to be beheaded for their crimes, while their Chinese accomplices would be put to death by strangulation. He then ordered the Cohong to pass along a command to the foreigners to turn over all of the thousands of chests of opium that were then being stored in ships at Lintin Island and elsewhere. He also ordered the foreigners (through the Cohong) to all sign pledges vowing never again to trade opium in China. Lin offered no form of compensation for the thousands of pounds of opium they were ordered to hand over.

At the same time that Lin was ordering the foreigners to turn over their opium supplies, he attempted to persuade them

COMMISSIONER LIN WRITES TO SUPERINTENDENT ELLIOT

Soon after Commissioner Lin Zexu ordered the British to turn their illegal opium over to the Chinese government, he wrote to Superintendent Charles Elliot, spelling out his reasons why this should be, and why Elliot should not encourage the traders to resist his demands:

> The Sovereign of your country will take strong measures against you on hearing of this. There have been many instances of British officials getting into serious trouble at home for disobeying Chinese regulations, as you must surely be aware. . . . [F]oreigners must surely dread the anger of Heaven, which cannot fail to punish them if they continue to ruin so many Chinese homes, and cause the death of so many opium smokers and dealers; for it has now been decided that the death penalty is to be inflicted for opium offences. Again, seafarers are in particular danger from thunderstorms and gales, dragons, crocodiles

of the immorality of their opium trade, just as he had done with the Chinese. He urged them to trade only in legitimate products such as tea, silk, and rhubarb, and to refrain from causing any additional harm to the Chinese people. The Kwangsi-Kwangtung governor general, Lin's close ally, had already optimistically told the British that "the smokers have all quit the habit and the dealers have dispersed. There is no more demand for the drug and henceforth no profit can be derived from the traffic."[4]

Lin went one step further and wrote a letter directly to Queen Victoria herself, appealing to the head of the British government to help the Chinese in getting rid of opium:

and the giant salamander; and Heaven, if offended, may well use these as instruments of punishment. . . .

[T]here is [also] the legal aspect of the matter. There is a clause in our Code which says that people from countries outside our sphere of influence are subject to the same penalties as the Chinese themselves. . . . By a special act of grace you are only being asked to hand over your opium and sign our undertaking never to bring opium again and to accept that if you are caught doing so you will be dealt with according to the law and the whole of your cargo will be confiscated. . . .

I ask you, where in the whole world is there a better port than Canton? Here you can buy rhubarb and tea, without which you could not exist; various kinds of silk, without which you could not make your textiles. . . . Are you going to let the port be closed and sacrifice all these things merely on account of opium? . . .

What reason have you to cling to something which you are not allowed to sell and which no one is allowed to buy?*

* Arthur Waley, *The Opium War Through Chinese Eyes*, London: Allen & Unwin, 1958, pp. 36–38.

There is a class of evil foreigner that makes opium and brings it for sale, tempting fools to destroy themselves merely in order to reap profit. Formerly the number of opium smugglers was small; but now the vice has spread far and wide, and the poison penetrated deeper. . . . We have decided to inflict very serious penalties on opium dealers and opium smokers. . . . This poisonous article is manufactured by certain devilish persons in places subject to your rule. It is not of course either made or sold at your bidding. . . . I am told that in your own country opium smoking is forbidden under severe penalties. . . . It would be better to forbid the sale of it, or better still to forbid the production of it. . . . What is here forbidden to consume, your dependencies must be forbidden to manufacture. . . . When that is done, not only will the Chinese be rid of this evil but your people too will be safe.[5]

What Lin did not know, of course, was that opium was not as yet prohibited in Britain, and his plea to Queen Victoria never reached her. Additional pressure would have to be used to force the British to turn over their opium and stop the trade forever.

FORCING THE BRITISH HAND

Initially, the British were determined to ignore Lin's order to turn over their stock of opium, despite the pleas of the Hong merchants, who would face severe punishment if the British did not obey Lin's orders. The British explained to the Cohong that the opium was not really theirs, but was just theirs to sell on consignment. When that argument failed to work, they offered to turn over to the merchants a token offering of 1,000 chests of opium, an insult that infuriated Lin even further.

In retaliation, Lin ordered the arrest of one of the leading British opium traders, Lancelot Dent, who himself controlled more than 6,000 chests of opium. Knowing that Dent faced execution by the Chinese, the British refused to turn him over

This detail of a relief sculpture depicts men, on orders from Lin Zexu, destroying opium chests in Canton. A Chinese official during the Qing dynasty, Lin sought to take the high moral ground in his battle against the opium trade in China.

to the Chinese to be put on trial. In response, Lin ordered the Hoppo to stop any and all foreign trade on March 24, 1839. All Chinese personnel were ordered to leave their foreign employers, and the 350 foreigners in Canton, including Superintendent Elliot, were sealed off in their Factories. For six weeks, the foreigners were trapped there, living on limited supplies of food and water, while the surrounding Chinese troops kept up a constant onslaught of noise with gongs and drums.

After these weeks of ordeal, the traders agreed to turn over 20,000 chests of opium to the queen's representative, Superintendent Elliot, who would in turn give it to the Chinese. The traders, by turning it over to the government, were promised that they would receive compensation from the government for their loss. With this agreement, Elliot was able to get trade (and that year's tea crop) moving, and the Chinese would win what looked like for them a considerable victory. It was, for all concerned, as good a win as could be expected.

Lin personally supervised the movement of the opium from British to Chinese hands, and he even lived on a boat during the months of April and May to prevent the possibility of either cheating or theft. After all 20,000 chests, amounting to nearly 3 million pounds (1.3 million kg) of raw opium, had been turned over, Lin ordered that three trenches, each 7 feet (2.1 m) deep and 150 feet (45.7 m) long, be dug. Under the watchful eye of 60 government officials, 500 workers broke up the large balls of raw opium and mixed them with water, salt, and lime until the opium had fully dissolved. Finally, as huge crowds watched, the sludge was flushed out into a small creek, and from there into the Southern Sea.

Lin offered a special prayer to the spirit of the Southern Sea, "you who wash away all stains and cleanse all impurities," and apologized for the fact that "poison has been allowed to creep in unchecked till at last barbarian smoke fills the market." He also wrote, regarding the foreigners who watched the destruction of the opium, that they "do not dare show any disrespect, and indeed I should judge from their attitudes that they have the decency to feel heartily ashamed."[6]

Indeed, as Jonathan D. Spence points out in his book *The Search for Modern China*, Lin and the emperor seemed to believe that the citizens of Canton and the foreign traders had "simple, childlike natures that would respond to firm guidance and statements of moral principles set out in simple, clear terms."[7] Like a parent punishing an unruly child, they hoped to show the opium users and traders, through some "tough love," the error of their ways.

This proved to be a catastrophic miscalculation. Destroying 3 million pounds (1.3 million kg) of opium on hand in Canton did not even begin to address the problem of the huge stockpiles of opium in India ready to be shipped into China. Too much money was at stake for the British to allow a momentary defeat to stop the opium trade altogether. Additionally, there was now the problem of who was going to compensate the British traders for their 20,000 destroyed chests of opium. Since it was the Chinese who destroyed it, it was, in the eyes of many British, the Chinese who should pay for it. The Chinese "victory" was about to turn into a defeat that would shake the country to its core.

Britain Flexes
Its Muscles

They had seen it asserted, over and over again, that the Government was advocating the cause of the contraband trade, in order to force an opium war on the public; but he thought it impossible to be conceived that a thought so absurd and atrocious should have entered the minds of the British Ministry.

—Thomas Babington Macaulay, Secretary for War,
in the Parliamentary Debate of April 7, 1840[1]

Superintendent Charles Elliot was more determined than ever to protect British interests in China, including the right to trade opium freely. He ordered all of his countrymen to leave Canton, depriving the Chinese of the opportunity of using them as hostages ever again. As of May 27, 1839, all British ships and most British citizens had left the

Pearl River for Macao. Two weeks later, on June 7, an armed merchant ship, the *Cambridge*, arrived in Macao. Its owner, James Douglas, was appointed by Elliot to be commodore of the British merchantmen who had left Canton and were now at anchor between Hong Kong Island and Kowloon, both districts of present-day Hong Kong.

Now in a stronger position than he had been just one month earlier, Elliot once again began to push back against Commissioner Lin. By mid-July, opium smuggling, coming from both Macao and the Spanish-controlled city of Manila, was once again in high gear all along the coast of Fukien (today known as Fujian), the birthplace of Commissioner Lin. The Chinese Navy was powerless to put a stop to it.

The British government also began to move into action, placing additional pressure on China. Elliot had already written to London asking for military assistance to be sent to China to be used if necessary. In full support of the British merchants, Foreign Secretary Lord Palmerston wrote a letter to "The Minister of the Emperor of China," expressing "extreme surprise" that Chinese officials had "committed violent outrages against the British Residents at Canton, who were living peaceably in that city, trusting to the good faith of the Chinese Government." Palmerston added that although the queen herself did not approve of opium selling, she "cannot permit that her subjects residing abroad be treated with violence, and be exposed to insult and injustice."[2]

Trade interests and diverse chambers of commerce began to place pressure on Parliament to take retaliatory action against China. William Jardine himself made the long journey from China to England to use whatever influence he had. It worked. Parliament, while not taking the full step of declaring war, did authorize sending a fleet and mobilizing additional troops in India in order to obtain "satisfaction and reparation."[3] The total force—16 gunships carrying 540 guns, 4 armed steamers, and 4,000 troops—was placed under the command of

Charles Elliot's cousin, Admiral George Elliot, along with 3,000 tons (2,721.5 metric tons) of coal for the steamers and 16,000 gallons (60,566.5 litres) of rum for the men. It would, however, take months for the fleet to arrive to back up Elliot and the British merchants.

In the meantime, Lin continued in his assigned task of wiping out the opium trade. Arrests continued, driving the price of a chest of opium to $3,000, up from an average $500. Tensions mounted on July 12 when a group of British seamen, at the Chinese village of Chien-sha-tsin on Kowloon peninsula, began their shore leave by destroying a Chinese temple and ending it by beating up a Chinese man named Lin Wei-hsi, who died the next day.

The problem facing Chinese authorities was a complicated one: Which of the sailors involved in the beating was to blame for Lin Wei-hsi's death? Elliot knew he faced a problem of his own and tried to resolve it by handing out money as quickly as he could—$1,500 for the dead man's family, $200 as a reward for evidence "convicting the real murderer," $100 for other villagers, and $400 as payment to local officials. The costs of Elliot's round of bribes were charged to the drug smuggling firms that used the ships involved in the murder.

Unsurprisingly, Commissioner Lin was furious about the murder and Elliot's bribes. Lin blanketed the streets of Macao with posters noting that if a Chinese person had killed a foreigner that person would immediately be executed, and he reiterated the Chinese principle that "he who kills a man must pay the penalty of life."

Elliot, however, had no intention of turning any Englishman, even one guilty of murder, over to the Chinese. Public opinion back home in Britain would never have stood for it. In an attempt to placate the Chinese, Elliot held a trial for the six most likely suspects aboard the ship *Fort William*. The trial became a mockery of justice when the murder charges against one of the accused, Thomas Tidder, were thrown out by a jury of British merchants, and five other seamen were convicted of nothing more than rioting and were given small fines and short prison sentences upon their return to Britain. When the sailors finally returned to Britain, the prison sentences were ignored.

Lin had had about enough of the British flouting Chinese laws. The last straw came when the British merchants, backed by Superintendent Elliot, once again refused to sign bonds promising not to deal in opium or face certain execution. With that, on August 17, 1839, Lin ordered the British to leave Macao. By August 25, all 57 families of the British community had left the Portuguese city and were living uncomfortably on ships in Hong Kong Harbor. "No doubt they have on their ships," Lin wrote the emperor, "a certain stock of dried provisions; but they will soon find themselves without the heavy, greasy meat dishes for which they have such a passion."[4] (The Chinese, who ate little or no red meat, were disgusted and amused by the large amounts of meat that the English ate on a regular basis.) Eventually, the British began the process of settling on the nearly deserted island of Hong Kong, which they would control for more than 150 years.

Lin, convinced that the British would soon use military force against China, began to fortify the waterways leading into Canton. He purchased new cannons for the forts, installed large chains to block the channel, and began training and drilling new military recruits. Five thousand tea porters were recruited and paid six dollars a month by the Cohong merchants, providing they could pass the physical test. They were required to lift over their heads a five-foot-long (1.5 m-long) pole with a granite wheel at each end, for a total of 133 pounds (60.3 kg). Fishermen as well were called upon to use their own boats to patrol and raid the new British settlements.

Such preparations were something new for the Chinese. As Jack Beeching pointed out in his book *The Chinese Opium Wars*, the idea of "war" between two nations was alien to the Chinese. While China had experienced raids from outside barbarians (such as the Manchus) and had suffered rebellions from within the country, it had never endured war with another nation. Indeed, "the one great moral justification for the Chinese Empire . . . had been that whatever its technical backwardness or social oppressiveness, within its own vast borders it kept the peace."[5]

WAR APPROACHES

The British in Hong Kong found themselves under the threat of constant harassment by local Chinese. Wells were poisoned and food proved nearly impossible to purchase. Minor clashes broke out between British ships and Chinese war junks in Hong Kong Harbor as well as in the Bogue outside Canton throughout September and October of 1839.

Ratcheting up the stakes, Lin, in a break from Chinese tradition, began to call for citizens to arm themselves and prepare for war. "Assemble yourselves together for consideration," said one proclamation. "Purchase arms and weapons; join together the stoutest of your villagers and thus be prepared to defend yourselves."[6] Although armed citizens had previously been thought to be a threat to the government and elite classes, Lin's call to arms seemed a necessity as the British Parliament began debate on the need for war with China.

PAYING A DEBT

Lord Palmerston was strongly in favor of the war. Not only was he anxious to push aside China's refusal to open up its borders to free trade, there was now the matter that the British government had lost £2 million when the British opium traders had turned their stock over to Elliot to be given to Lin to be destroyed. The traders had only done so with the promise that they would be compensated for their loss. Where was the money in compensation to come from? While Lord Palmerston did not think he would be able to persuade Parliament to vote to approve the funds, there was one other possibility.

What if China could be forced to pay the money itself? What if a war in China could be made to pay for itself by forcing China, after its inevitable defeat, to pay the British compensation for the opium destroyed and for the cost of the war itself? The military force that Elliot had requested was already well on its way to China. Getting Parliament to vote for a war under those circumstances would prove to be a fairly easy fight.

There were those in Parliament who were opposed to the opium trade, who felt that Britain was undermining its own moral authority by its involvement in the drug trade. One of those most strongly opposed was William Gladstone, then a member of Parliament who would go on to become British prime minister on four separate occasions. Gladstone's own sister, Helen, had been given laudanum for a minor ailment while still young and had become a hopeless opium addict by the age of 24. So when Gladstone addressed the House of Commons on the question of war with China, his views were intensified by his own personal experience:

> They [the Chinese] gave you notice to abandon your contraband trade. When they found you would not do so they had the right to drive you from their coasts on account of your obstinacy in persisting with this infamous and atrocious traffic. . . . Justice, in my opinion, is with them; and whilst they, the Pagans, the semi-civilized barbarians, have it on their side, we, the enlightened and civilized Christians, are pursuing objects at variance both with justice and with religion. . . . A war more unjust in its origin, a war calculated in its progress to cover this country with a permanent disgrace, I do not know and I have not read of.[7]

It was an incredibly effective speech, but Lord Palmerston had the final word. He read on the floor a memorial from American merchants in Canton, who had written the U.S. Congress asking for a joint naval force from Britain, France, and the United States to take action against China. The memorial made it appear that the problem was the not opium trade per se, but was bringing China to act in line with the rest of the "civilized" world.

Palmerston also informed the House of Commons of a petition that he had received, signed by the representatives of the most important British companies trading in China, that stated that "unless measures of the government are followed up with firmness and energy, the trade with China can no longer be conducted with security to life and property, or with credit or advantage to the British nation."[8] The fact that the first signature on the petition was that of William Jardine, perhaps the most successful of the opium traders, proved beside the point. Parliament voted to approve war against China. In June 1840, the British fleet under George Elliot arrived in Canton. The players were now all in place for the war to begin.

With the arrival of military force, the opium trade, which had slowed down to a crawl, quickly picked up steam. Under the British fleet's protection, the receiving ships once again waited at Lintin for Chinese galleys to pick up supplies and to bring the drug ashore, now in broad daylight. Opium prices were published in the *Canton Register*. Wherever there was an opium clipper, a ship from the British fleet was sure to be there to protect it.

In the meantime, Commissioner Lin remained dedicated to stomping out opium addiction in China. In May 1840, Lin established a refuge, what would today be called a rehab center, outside of the Gate of Eternal Purity (the gate that led directly to Canton's execution ground), for opium users who wanted to break the habit. The techniques used then were rough and rudimentary compared with the ones used at modern rehab clinics such as the Betty Ford Center. Addicts were placed in solitary confinement and given a course of pills that was supposed to make breaking the addiction easier. The Chinese believed that addicts should be given every opportunity to achieve a cure of their illness. As Beeching writes, however, a harsh end awaited "those who are unwilling, or cannot leave off, must wait till they die of the disease they themselves have engendered."[9]

In this 1843 illustration by Henry Adlard, the British attack on and capture of Chuenpee, near Canton, China, in January 1841, is shown.

To help lift the spirits of his men, and in the hopes of capturing some hostages, Lin posted a list of bounties available to his army. If someone were to succeed in sinking a 74-gun ship, the reward would be the equivalent of $20,000, an enormous amount of money at that time. If someone were to capture a naval commander alive, the reward would be $5,000; dead, only a third of that. Commissioner Elliot himself was worth $50,000. British military men were worth $100 each. The Sepoys, however—Indian troops in the British service—were worth only $20 each.

Much to Lin's chagrin, when the British finally attacked, they avoided his newly built defenses around Canton. Instead, leaving four ships behind to block the entrance to the harbor, the bulk of their force sailed north. In July 1840, the British blockaded the coastal city of Ningbo with two ships, and then

proceeded to capture the main town on the island of Chou-
shan (also known as Zhoushan) off the Chekiang (today
known as Zheijiang) coast. With this move, the British were
now in a position to control all sea traffic going in and out of
the Chang (also known as Yangzi) River delta region. This was
a considerable advantage, since the Chang is China's longest
and most important river system.

Leaving a military force behind (along with a missionary-
interpreter who stood in for the Qing magistrate who committed suicide after his city was conquered), the British sailed on
to the mouth of the Bei He (or North River), near the Dagu

SONGS OF OH DEAR, OH DEAR!

After the British captured Chen-hai and Ningbo in October
1841, a call went out for new Chinese recruits to participate
in the Chinese counterattack. At the city of Soochow (today
known as Suzhou), mandarins, merchants, and students were
encouraged to join. One hundred and forty-four men responded, including a 30-year-old poet named Pei Ch'ing-ch'iao,
whose father urged him to enlist. He recalled:

> My father was fond of talking about military matters. He had
> formerly served on the staff of Lu K'un (1772–1835). But it
> had not fallen to his lot to accompany Lu either during the
> campaign against the Moslem leader Jehangir or during that
> against the Yao aborigines. My father mentioned how much it
> weighed upon his mind that he had missed these campaigns.
> When the English foreigners began their havoc in Fuhkien
> and Chekiang I expressed my indignation by writing a set of
> nine poems. My father read them and said, "If you feel so
> strongly about it, why don't you join the army?" Upon this I
> went straight to headquarters and offered my services.*

forts that guarded the approaches to the major city of Tientsin. With the British now controlling China's main northern waterways, the governor-general of the region, Qishan, saw that it was time to negotiate with the British.

The negotiations continued through August and September 1840. Qishan, a senior Manchu and a grand secretary who had earned the trust of Emperor Daoguang, persuaded the British to leave northern China and return to Canton to finish negotiating, an accomplishment for which he was later honored by the emperor by being named governor-general of Kwangsi and Kwangtung. Commissioner Lin, who had been named to

When Pei Ch'ing-ch'iao was on his way to war, his father presented him with a sword as well as a poem warning him that unless he used it to cut off the head of a foreign chieftain, he would not be welcome to return home.

Unfortunately for Pei, his sword was of little use to him. Instead, when the war ended, he wrote one of the few existing accounts of the war as seen through the eyes of a low-ranking staff officer, which took the form of a series of poems interspersed with long sections of prose, a traditional literary form in China. The title of his book, *Tu-tu Yin*, means "Songs of Oh dear, Oh dear!" and is a reference to the story of the fourth-century general Yin Hao. Yin, after he was cashiered, or expelled, from the army, reportedly spent his remaining days just sitting, tracing with his finger in the air the words, "Oh dear, Oh dear, what an odd business!"**

---

* Arthur Waley, *The Opium War Through Chinese Eyes*, London: Allen & Unwin, 1958, pp. 159-160.
** Ibid.

that position at the beginning of 1840, was now dismissed in disgrace for his failures and banished to Ili, in the northwest section of China.

In January 1841, Qishan reached a final settlement with the British. The British could give back to China the island of Chou-shan, but in return were officially given control over Hong Kong. In addition, Qishan agreed that China would pay $6 million to the British, would grant the British direct official contact with the Chinese government, and that Canton trade would be reopened to them within 10 days of signing the agreement. Apparently, these concessions went far beyond what Emperor Daoguang was prepared to accept. Furious with Qishan, he ordered him dismissed and executed; the death sentence was later commuted to banishment.

Ironically, Lord Palmerston was just as furious with Charles Elliot, but in this case for not winning better terms from the Chinese. He wrote to Elliot in April 1841 (it took three months for the news of the agreement to reach London), dismissing him from his position and refusing to ratify the agreement. He told Elliot, "You have disobeyed and neglected your instructions; you have deliberately abstained from employing, as you might have done, the force placed at your disposal; and you have without any sufficient necessity accepted terms which fall far short of those which you were instructed to obtain."[10]

Even Queen Victoria attacked her one-time representative, saying that Charles Elliot "completely disobeyed his instructions and *tried* to get the *lowest* terms he could."[11] For his part, Elliot defended his actions. Upon returning to London he published a memorandum that said in part, "It has been popularly objected to me that I have cared too much for the Chinese. But I submit that it has been caring more for lasting British honor and substantial British interests to protect a helpless and friendly people."[12] (Interestingly, within a year, Charles Elliot, thanks to family connections, had received a new assignment as the British consul-general to the Republic of Texas, a nation that would become part of the United States in 1845.)

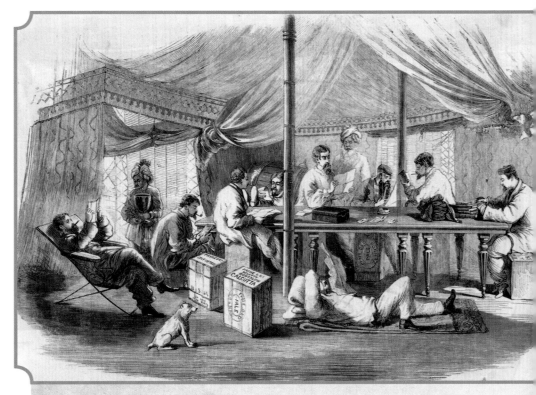

Indian officers of the 15th Punjabees are seen relaxing in their tent at Pehtang during the First Opium War between Britain and China. The British used Indian soldiers, called Sepoys, to fight in China.

Unfortunately for Elliot and those who agreed with his stance, the days of "caring" for the Chinese people were long over. A new representative, Sir Henry Pottinger, was sent to China to finish the job that Elliot could not. In his instructions to Pottinger, Lord Palmerston insisted that any agreement with China must be with the emperor himself: "Her Majesty's Government cannot allow that, in a transaction between Great Britain and China, the unreasonable practice of the Chinese should supersede the reasonable practice of all the rest of mankind."[13] In other words, no matter what China's wishes might be, it would be forced to open its doors to open trade and work directly with the British government, like it or not.

When Pottinger arrived in China in August 1841, he discovered that the situation had grown more tense and unpredictable. There had been fighting in the countryside surrounding Canton, and numerous British troops had been killed and wounded. In response, the British had destroyed the Bogue Forts, sank a large number of Chinese junks, and had begun occupying sections of Canton. The British troops later withdrew from Canton after officials of that city paid them the equivalent of $6 million to do so. It remains unclear whether this money was a ransom paid for their city, an attempt to equal the money paid to Elliot earlier regarding Qishan, or payback for the destroyed opium of two years earlier.

Perhaps in response to the renewed British display of force, the prefect of Canton came down to Macao on August 18, along with an official escort, to greet the new representative of the queen. This concession to British strength did little good though, as Pottinger was determined to bring the war to a quick and conclusive end.

A QUICK WAR

Pottinger moved quickly. By the end of August, he had traveled north with the British fleet, capturing the coastal cities of Amoy (Xiamen) and Ningbo, and easily recapturing Chou-shan. From Chou-shan, there were two ways to attack deep into the heart of China. One possibility was the route that the Chinese authorities predicted the British would go—directly toward Peking. The problem with that plan, however, was that the Pei-ho River, the direct path to Peking, was so shallow that few of the large British ships would be able to use it.

The other possibility was easier from the British point of view. Almost 200 miles (321.8 km) up the Chang River lay the city of Nanking (Nanjing). Near Nanking ran the Great Canal, by which the rice grown in Central China was carried by junks to feed the nearly 3 million inhabitants of Peking. By threatening to cut off the food supply to Peking, it was hoped that the emperor would be more than willing to come to terms with British demands.

When fresh Sepoy reinforcements reached Pottinger from India in late spring of 1842, he proceeded with this strategy. British troops captured Shanghai in June and Chekiang the following month. The Manchus fought back hard, but to no avail. Armed primarily with pikes, knives, and spears, they found themselves powerless against the latest British percussion muskets and overwhelming naval superiority. Even a half-hearted plan to throw monkeys carrying fireworks into the sails of docked British warships proved a failure. As if that were not enough, on July 8, 1842, China observed a total eclipse of the sun—to the Chinese, a sign of national disaster.

As the British war machine rolled on, scores of Manchu officers murdered their own wives and children by strangulation, poison, or by the sword, before killing themselves in despair. By September 5, the British had put up announcements throughout Chekiang, announcing that peace negotiations had begun. At the same time, the war-shocked inhabitants of the city were informed that by traveling to Chou-shan they would find "opium is on sale very cheap—an opportunity not to be missed."[14] The opium traders following the British Royal Navy up the Chang River were ready to do business.

Despite pronouncements that peace negotiations were taking place, Pottinger's forces were still moving up the river, ignoring the Qing requests for talks. By August 5, troops had positioned themselves outside the former Ming dynasty capital of Nanking, a city as large as Paris, surrounded by 30 miles (48.2 km) of sandstone walls. Facing certain defeat, citizens in the city raised a large white flag. Emperor Daoguang sent three commissioners to Nanjing to negotiate on his behalf, as the Qing dynasty decided that the time had come to sue for peace. The First Opium War—and with it China's ability to resist the power of the British Empire—had come to an end.

The Treaty of Nanking and Afterward

Remarkably, given China's overwhelming defeat by the British, the emperor's representatives wrote back to him with a spirit of optimism, suggesting that they were negotiating from a position of strength and that placating the British would do the trick: "Should we fail to . . . ease the situation by soothing the barbarians, they will run over our country like beasts, doing anything they like."[1] It turned out that "soothing the barbarians" meant giving in to nearly all of their demands.

On August 29, 1842, the Treaty of Nanking was signed aboard the HMS *Cornwallis* moored in the Chang River. The document, written in both English and Chinese, was first signed by Sir Henry Pottinger. Then the three commissioners sent by the emperor signed the agreement without taking the time to read it. (I-li-pu, one of the Chinese commissioners who had signed the treaty, was so shamed by his nation's defeat and

A picture of the Treaty of Nanking, under which China ceded the island of Hong Kong to Great Britain in 1842. The two nations' representatives who signed the treaty were Chi Ying of China and Sir Henry Pottinger of Great Britain.

his part in its surrender that he asked the emperor to punish him for giving in to the English. He was later banished as a common criminal.) After cherry brandy toasts to Queen Victoria were offered, as well as the Chinese tradition of eating sugarplums, the ceremony was completed. Ten months later it was ratified in Hong Kong after receiving formal approval from Queen Victoria and Emperor Daoguang.

The treaty itself, consisting of 12 major articles, clearly spelled out a new relationship between Britain and China. These changes had long-term ramifications for China's concepts of commerce, society, and its place in the international community.

Article 1 laid down the concept of peace and friendship between Britain and China and "full security and protection for their persons and property within the dominions of the other."[2] Article 2 established that five Chinese cities—Canton, Foochow, Xiamen, Ningbo, and Shanghai, would be opened up to residence by British subjects and their families "for the purpose of carrying on their mercantile pursuits, without molestation or restraint."[3] It also allowed for the opening of a formal consulate in each city. Article 3 ensured that the "Island of Hong Kong to be possessed in perpetuity"[4] by Queen Victoria and her successors, to be ruled as they "shall see fit."[5]

The next several articles dealt with financial issues. Article 4 provided payment of $6 million by the Qing for the opium that was destroyed in Canton. Article 5 ensured that the Canton Cohong monopoly system was abolished, and British merchants in Canton, Foochow, Amoy, Ningbo, and Shanghai were granted permission "to carry on their mercantile transactions with whatever persons they please."[6] Additionally, the Qing were obligated to pay $3 million in settlement of outstanding Cohong debts. Article 6 guaranteed that the British were to be paid an additional $12 million "on account of the expenses incurred"[7] in the war. In Article 7, the total of $21 million that was ordered to be paid in Articles 4 through 6 described how the money was to be paid in four installments before the end of 1845. A 5 percent interest charge per year would be added for any late payments.

The latter articles primarily pertained to the treatment of British subjects and Chinese citizens who had been allied with the British during the war. Article 8 declared that any British subjects, whether Indian or European, were to be immediately released from prison. Article 9 granted amnesty to any Chinese subjects who had either lived with, did business with, or in any way served or helped the British. Article 10 explained that at each of the five treaty ports opened up to the British, merchants would only pay a "fair and regular Tariff of Export and Import

Customs and other Dues."[8] Article 11 explained how, instead of terms such as "petition" or "beg" that foreigners had traditionally been forced to use, new, nonsubordinate terms of address such as "communication," "statement," and "declaration" were to be used in all formal communication between Britain and China.[9] Finally, Article 12 described how after the British received the first payment of money owed from China, British forces would leave Nanking and the Grand Canal and "no longer molest or stop the trade of China."[10] Troops would remain in Chou-shan until all payments had been made and the five named ports had officially been opened to British merchants.

Reading the summaries of the articles from the treaty, it is clear there is one thing missing: No cause of war has been included. There is no mention, outside of the $6 million payment for the opium destroyed in 1839, of opium or the opium trade itself. When the treaty was being negotiated, Pottinger did bring up the matter with the chief Manchu negotiator, Qiying, remarking only that the British government hoped that the Qing would allow opium to be legalized on a barter basis. When Qiying replied that he could not possibly bring up that proposal with the emperor, however, Pottinger did not push the point, stating only that he had been ordered not to press the issue.

It was the only "victory" the Chinese managed to eke out of the treaty negotiations. The payments due to the British, totaling $21 million, were equal to half of the entire Chinese revenue of any one year, causing extreme damage to the nation's economy. Additionally, China was no longer able to ignore the wishes of the "barbarians" who wished to do business in their country, especially not with five cities now completely open to trade.

On top of that, other nations pressured China to give them the same rights and privileges that it had given the British. Treaties were signed with the United States and France, allowing both nations trading rights, allowing American Protestant

Treaty Ports and Towns and Boxer Rebellion, 1842–1911

N

Sakhalin I.

Lake Baikal

▲ Aigun

Amur R.

▲ Manchouli

Sui-fen ▲

MANCHURIA

Hun-ch'un ▲

Sea of Japan

Ch'ang-ch'un

Mukden ▲ Antung

Newchwang ◻ ▲

JAPAN

Tianjin ◻

Yellow Sea

Huang He

CHINA

Chinkiang

Nanjing ▲ ◻ ▲ Wusung

Wuhu ● ○ Shanghai

Soochow ▲

Hankow ◻ Hangchow ▲ ○ Ningpo

Yangtze R. ◻ Wenchow ○

Ichang ● Kiukiang

Chongqing ▲ ▲ Yochow

Changsha Santu-ao ▲

Fuzhou ○ ◻ Tamsul

Amoy ○ *Formosa*

East China Sea

PACIFIC OCEAN

Tengyueh ▲

Manhao Canton Swatow

Szemao ▲ ◻ (Guangzhou) ○ ◻

Mengtze ◻ Nanning ▲ ▲ Kowloon

Lungchow ◻ ○ Pakhoi

Ch'iung-chou ◻

Hainan

Mekong R.

South China Sea

© Infobase Learning

| | Area of the Boxer Rebellion, 1900–11 |

Ports and Towns Opened to Trade

○ 1842	● 1876
◻ 1858	◻ 1897
△ 1860	▲ 1911

0 ——— 300 miles
0 ——— 300 km

This map shows the treaty ports and towns opened to European trade by China as a result of European military pressure. The shaded area represents the extent of the Boxer Rebellion.

missionaries the right to build churches and hospitals, and allowing both nations the right to be judged by their own national laws rather than Chinese law while in China. These new rights were also given over to the British, courtesy of an additional treaty signed between Great Britain and China in 1843. This new treaty included a stipulation that any rights and privileges given by the emperor to any subject or citizen of any other country would also be given to the British as well.

As Jonathan D. Spence wrote, "[W]ithin six years of Lin Zexu's appointment as imperial commissioner, the Qing, instead of defending their integrity against all comers, had lost control of vital elements of China's commercial, social, and foreign policies."[11] The time of China as the "Celestial Kingdom," the "Middle Kingdom," as a nation that could ignore the rest of the world as it so pleased, as a nation that was in sole control of its destiny, was now over.

AFTER THE WAR

Although initially none of the foreign merchants gained as much as they had hoped from the opening of Chinese ports to trade, the opium trade itself continued to be very profitable, with more than 20,000 chests arriving per year, despite its continued illegality. Shanghai, however, soon became a financial boomtown, as British, French, and other foreign settlements sprang up along the recently drained riverside. While only 44 foreign ships had entered the port in 1844, that number had risen to 437 by 1855; at the same time, the silk trade grew to more than $20 million annually by the mid-1850s.

Despite (or perhaps because of) the newly signed treaty, tensions continued to grow between the Chinese and the growing number of foreign merchants. The 1840s through to the early 1850s witnessed frequent rioting in the cities and continuing anti-British attacks by rural militias. Violence rose against the Qing itself as Chinese citizens, angered by the corruption and weakness of the dynasty—evidenced by its inability to protect the country from foreign "barbarians"—rebelled against the emperor. The Taiping Rebellion, a large-scale revolt that began in 1850 and ended in 1871, further weakened the Qing. Over the course of those years, 20 million to 30 million were killed in the rebellion before government forces eventually crushed it.

THE SECOND OPIUM WAR

Given its weakened position, the Qing dynasty was in no position to fight another war against the British, but fight it did, in what has become known as the Second Opium War (1856–1860). What started as a simple incident regarding piracy and smuggling on a British registered ship, the *Arrow*, on October 8, 1856, grew into another devastating loss for the Chinese.

The British moved to attack Canton from the Pearl River. At the same time, bakers in Hong Kong attempted to poison the entire European community by lacing bread with arsenic. While the conspiracy was discovered and tragedy was averted, when the news reached London, anger against the Chinese grew into a call for war. The call was joined by the French government, which was angered by the execution of a French missionary, Father Auguste Chapdelaine.

In late 1857, the combined British and French forces attacked and occupied Canton. The coalition then cruised north to briefly capture the Taku Forts near Tientsin in May 1858, which led to the signing of the Treaties of Tientsin in June of that year. The major parts were:

1. Britain, France, Russia, and the United States would have the right to establish diplomatic legations in Peking, a city that was closed to foreigners at the time.
2. Ten additional Chinese ports would be opened for foreign trade.
3. All foreign vessels had the right to navigate freely on the Chang River.

4. All foreigners had the right to travel freely in the internal regions of China.

5. China was to pay an indemnity to Britain and France of 2 million taels (a Chinese measurement weight) of silver each.

6. China was to pay compensation to British merchants in 2 million taels of silver to pay for loss of property.

Once again, China had been defeated, and once again, China was forced to open its doors even wider to foreign influence. The worst, however, was still to come. Urged on by hawkish ministers, Emperor Xianfeng grew determined to stop the foreigners from moving up the river to his capital city of Peking. So, on June 2, 1858, the emperor ordered troops to guard the Dagu Fort in Tientsin and to reinforce the forts with added artillery. When a British naval force sailed to the mouth of the Hai River guarded by the Dagu Fort and demanded to proceed to Peking, fighting broke out, and four British gunboats were lost and two others severely damaged.

The British and French had had enough of Chinese resistance. Combined forces from both countries landed at Bei Tang, approximately two miles (3.2 km) from the Dagu Fort, on August 3, and began moving inland, fighting determined Chinese military resistance all along the way. On September 21, at the Battle of Palikao, Mongolian General Sengee Rinchen's 10,000 troops were wiped out by the combined Anglo-French forces. On October 6, British and French troops entered the Chinese capital city of Peking.

With his army devastated, Emperor Xianfeng fled the capital, leaving his brother, Prince Gong, in charge of negotiations. For a time, the British considered destroying the Forbidden City, the then-450-year-old seat of the emperor's power, as revenge against Chinese transgressions. Instead, on October 18, after days of looting, the British command ordered the burning of the emperor's Summer Palace. It was at this time that the gifts of Lord Macartney, given to Emperor Qianlong in 1793, were discovered in storage, still unused.

The Qing was now powerless to stand up to the demands of the British and French. On October 18, 1860, the abdicated emperor's brother, Yixin, finally ratified the Treaties of Tientsin and signed the additional Convention of Peking, ending the Second Opium War. Under the Convention of Peking, all official Chinese documents had to be written in English. The Chinese were forced to pay an additional 6 million pieces of silver to Britain and France. Britain also gained control of Jiulong (next to Hong Kong). At last, the opium trade was now formally legalized in China. Seventy-nine years after Warren Hastings sent his first shipment of opium to Canton, after years of Chinese resistance, after two deadly and costly wars, the British were now free to legally bring opium into China. The list of requests that Lord Macartney had presented to Emperor Qianlong in 1793 had finally been fulfilled.

AFTERMATH

For the Chinese, their humiliation was complete. The defeat of their imperial army by a small Anglo-British military force (outnumbered at least 10 to 1 by the Manchu army), coupled with the flight (and subsequent death) of the emperor and the burning of the Summer Palace, was a shocking blow to the once powerful Qing dynasty. As Immanuel Chung-yueh Hsu wrote: "Beyond a doubt, by 1860 the ancient civilization that was China had been thoroughly defeated and humiliated by the West."[12]

The next 50 years saw the Qing dynasty continue its slow decline. Forced to legalize opium usage, China saw a surge in imports (6,700 tons [6,078 metric tons] in 1879) and an explosion of domestic production. By 1906, China was producing nearly 85 percent of the world's opium, some 35,000 tons a year. It is estimated that nearly 27 percent of its male population was addicted: 13.5 million addicts were consuming 39,000 tons of opium yearly. Even the British finally realized that there was a problem, and from 1880 on attempted to discourage the use of opium in China, but to no avail.

The Qing dynasty was powerless to do anything. Unable and unwilling to reform, it faced threats from the outside (war with Japan in 1894–1895) and rebellions from within. It was apparent to all except the Qing that the days for Manchu rule over China were coming to an end. Finally, on February 12, 1912, the last emperor, the six-year-old Puyi, was forced to abdicate. Two hundred and fifty-six years of Qing leaders, and nearly 2,000 years of imperial rule, had come to an end.

What came in its place was decades of chaos. Warlords, famines, civil war, and the Japanese invasion of China during World War II all played a role in the near collapse of Chinese society, until finally, on October 1, 1949, Mao Zedong, the chairman of the Communist Party of China, stood at the Gate of Heavenly Peace leading into the Forbidden City, the site of Chinese power, and declared to all the world the establishment of the People's Republic of China.

CHINA AND THE WORLD

With the rise of Mao's Communists in China, it was almost as if the previous hundred years had never happened. Foreign investments came to a near halt as China once again withdrew from the Western world (with the exception of other Communist countries) behind what became known as the "Bamboo Curtain." Under Mao's rule, China was, for the first time in nearly a century, a unified and sovereign nation. Living standards improved for many, but not all, of China's citizens.

Mao's government is credited today with eradicating both the consumption and production of opium by using a combination of repression and social reform during the 1950s. Ten million addicts were forced into compulsory treatment, dealers were executed, and opium-producing regions were planted

(continues on page 104)

ZENG GUOFAN AND THE STEAMSHIP

In the aftermath of defeats in the First and Second Opium Wars and the Taiping Rebellion that followed, many Chinese scholars and bureaucrats began a lengthy period of doubt and self-examination, hoping to find ways to restore China to its former power and greatness. One of these men was Zeng Guofan.

His approach was two-pronged. Zeng called for a renewal of traditional values and morals. He hoped to encourage students to once again take the traditional exams and study a strict Confucian curriculum. He worked to restore order to agricultural work, and to help resettle the millions of refugees whose lives had been disrupted by years of foreign invasion and domestic rebellion.

Zeng, however, while looking to the past for inspiration and values, was also one to look forward as well. He realized that China had no chance of recovering unless it began to embrace the best that the West had to offer. He argued that China must learn to strengthen itself by including foreign languages, mathematics, and science in its classrooms.

Others felt the same way. Noting that China was 100 times larger than France and 200 times larger than Great Britain, the influential scholar Feng Guifen wrote: "Why are they small and yet strong? Why are we large and yet weak?"* The answer, both men felt, lay in the skills that foreigners had in using their manpower resources, exploiting their agricultural capability to its fullest, strengthening the bond between ruler and subject, and ensuring that they were able to back up their words with action. To do that, Feng argued, China would need to learn to build strong ships and effective guns.

Zeng agreed, and he directed his staff to begin the process of building a steamboat. They failed, so Zeng ordered a young man on his staff, Yung Wing, to travel to the United States to purchase the machinery necessary for China to start manufacturing its own military equipment. It was not Yung's first trip to America. He had been educated at missionary schools in Macao and Hong Kong, before going to the United States in 1847. There, after three years of prep school, Yung entered Yale University and received his B.A. in 1854, the first Chinese to graduate from an American university.

Yung arrived back in the United States in the spring of 1864. With the country fighting a long and bloody Civil War, he found it difficult to find an American company that was able and willing to sell the equipment he wanted, but finally the Putnam Machine Company in Fitchburg, Massachusetts, agreed to fill his order. Leaving an American engineer to supervise the details, Yung began his trip back to China via San Francisco; Hawaii; and Yokohama, Japan. The equipment itself was shipped directly from New York to Shanghai.

Zeng Guofan first saw the completed machine tools at a new arsenal near Shanghai. According to Yung Wing, Zeng "stood and watched [the machine's] automatic movement with unabashed delight, for this was the first time he had seen machinery and how it worked."** Initially, the machines were used to manufacture guns and cannons. By 1868, however, a team of Western technicians helped to combine a Chinese-built hull and boiler with a rebuilt foreign steam engine. With that, the SS *Tianqi* ("The Auspicious") was launched. The move to modernization had finally begun.

---

*Jonathan D. Spence. *The Search for Modern China*, New York: W.W. Norton, 1990, p. 198.

**Ibid.

President Richard M. Nixon of the United States stands with Vice Premier Li Shiennian of China, looking out over the Great Wall during the president's trip to China in 1972. The trip helped to normalize relations between the United States and the People's Republic of China.

(continued from page 101)
with new crops. All this progress did, however, come at a high cost. The government controlled nearly every aspect of each citizen's life, dissent was not tolerated, and millions of Chinese died in famines, in prisons, and during periods of turmoil such as the Cultural Revolution.

Eventually, though, Chinese interest in the outside world grew. In 1972, President Richard M. Nixon of the United States traveled to China, making the trip to visit Mao in a way not dissimilar to that of Lord Macartney visiting Emperor Qianlong 180 years earlier. Since Mao's death in 1976, China has once again opened itself up to foreign investment—but once again only under its own terms—and has become one of the world's most powerful nations and an economic powerhouse.

During roughly this same period of time, from the early- to mid-twentieth century, the once mighty British Empire, which by its peak in 1922 held dominion over 450 million people, then a quarter of the world's population, and over territory that covered 13 million square miles (33.6 million square kilometers), began its own decline. Britain, exhausted by fighting two world wars and facing independence movements throughout its empire, began the process of granting independence to its colonies. In 1947, Britain granted its most populated and valuable property, India, its independence.

By 1981, the British Empire, with the exception of just a few scattered islands (such as the Falklands off the coast of Argentina), had nearly come to an end. In 1982, Prime Minister Margaret Thatcher of Great Britain traveled to the People's Republic of China to negotiate the future of Britain's sole remaining major colony, Hong Kong. This once empty island, given over to Britain as part of the terms of the Treaty of Nanking, had become one of the world's leading financial capitals, as well as a business and cultural hub for all of Asia.

Hong Kong Island itself had been given over to Britain "in perpetuity" under the terms of the Treaty of Nanking. The vast majority of the colony, however, was situated on the so-called New Territories, land and island not part of either Hong Kong or Kowloon, which had been acquired by Britain under a 99-year lease in 1898, a lease due to expire in 1997. Thatcher went to China hoping to persuade the Chinese leadership to allow Britain to continue administering the island while the Chinese held technical sovereignty.

Britain, however, was no longer in a position to dictate terms to China, and China was not willing to share control of Hong Kong with Britain. In 1984, a deal was reached. Under the terms of the Sino-British Joint Declaration, Hong Kong would become a Special Administrative Region of the People's

Republic of China and allowed to maintain its own ways for 50 years before being fully integrated into China.

The handover ceremony was held in 1997. It was, to the British, the end of an empire. To the Chinese, however, it held a different meaning: It was the end of what many had called the century of humiliation. With the Sino-British Joint Declaration, and the return of Macao by Portugal in 1999, China was now fully in control of its own territory for the first time since the Treaty of Nanking. The humiliations of that treaty had been erased, and China had become a part of the world community. This time, however, it was joining on its own terms. It was a new era.

CHRONOLOGY

1516	Portuguese first arrive in China.
1689	British begin to trade at Canton.
1715	First East India Company Factory is established at Canton.
1729	Emperor Yongzheng issues first edict against opium.
1757	Foreign trade is limited to Canton.
1793	Lord Macartney meets Emperor Qianlong in Peking.
1796	Edict prohibits opium smoking in China.
1800-1820	Opium imports into China reach about 5,000 chests per year.
1816	Lord Amherst goes to Peking.
1820	Facing competition from other sources, East India Company cuts price of opium, increases production.
1821	Tea trade is stopped in an attempt to enforce opium ban.
1831	Opium imports reach 19,000 chests per year.
1834	The trading monopoly for the East India Company ends; Napier's Fizzle.
1836	Captain Charles Elliot becomes Britain's chief superintendent of trade; opium imports increase to more than 80,000 chests.
1839	Commissioner Lin destroys opium at Canton; naval action in the Pearl River Delta effectively begins war.

1840   Main city on Chou-shan Island is captured.

1841   Canton is ransomed; Sir Henry Pottinger arrives as plenipotentiary, replacing Elliot; Amoy and Ningbo are captured.

1842   Shanghai is occupied; Chekiang is captured; Treaty of Nanking is signed, opening up China to foreign trade and giving Britain control of Hong Kong.

1850-1871   The Taipan Rebellion takes place throughout China, weakening the Qing Dynasty and killing between 20 and 30 million Chinese.

1856-1860   The Second Opium War, resulting in another defeat for the Chinese.

TIMELINE

1820
Facing competition from other sources, East India Company cuts price of opium, increases production.

1689
British begin to trade at Canton.

1689

1820

1729
Emperor Yongzheng issues first edict against opium.

1800–1820
Opium imports into China reach about 5,000 chests per year.

1796
Edict prohibits opium smoking in China.

1860   October 18 British troops burn down the emperor's summer palace.

1912   February 12 The last emperor, the six-year-old Puyi, abdicates, ending 256 years of Qing leaders' rule, and nearly 2,000 years of imperial rule.

1949   October 1 Mao Zedong, the chairman of the Communist Party of China, declares the establishment of the People's Republic of China.

1972   President Richard M. Nixon of the United States visits the People's Republic of China and meets with Mao Zedong, signaling the beginning of a new period of Chinese interest in the outside world.

1997   Great Britain returns Hong Kong to Chinese control.

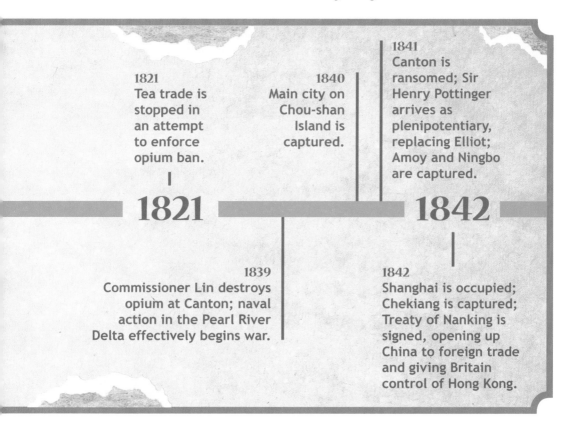

1821
Tea trade is stopped in an attempt to enforce opium ban.

1840
Main city on Chou-shan Island is captured.

1841
Canton is ransomed; Sir Henry Pottinger arrives as plenipotentiary, replacing Elliot; Amoy and Ningbo are captured.

1821   **1842**

1839
Commissioner Lin destroys opium at Canton; naval action in the Pearl River Delta effectively begins war.

1842
Shanghai is occupied; Chekiang is captured; Treaty of Nanking is signed, opening up China to foreign trade and giving Britain control of Hong Kong.

NOTES

CHAPTER 1

1. Julia Lovell, *The Great Wall: China Against the World, 1000 BC–AD 2000*. New York: Grove Press, 1975, p. 3.
2. Peter Ward Fay, *The Opium War: 1840–1842*, New York: W.W. Norton, 1975, p. 32.
3. Jack Beeching, *The Chinese Opium Wars*. New York: Harcourt Brace Jovanovich, 1975, p. 17.
4. Jonathan D. Spence, *The Search for Modern China*. New York: W.W. Norton, 1990, p. 123.
5. Ibid.
6. Beeching, p. 21.
7. Ibid., p. 18.

CHAPTER 2

1. Spence, p. 7.
2. Ibid.
3. Ibid., p. 3.
4. "The Ming Dynasty's Maritime History." http://www.ucalgary.ca/applied_history/tutor/eurvoya/ming.html.
5. Spence, pp. 22–23.
6. Ibid., p. 28.
7. Wei Chun, *On Ricci's Fallacies to Deceive the World*, quoted in George H.C. Wong, "China's Opposition to Western Science During Late Ming and Early Ch'ing," *Isis* 54, No. 1. (March 1963), pp. 22–49 (44).
8. Spence, p. 120.

CHAPTER 3

1. "East India Company." Microsoft Encarta Online Encyclopedia 2008.
2. "Indian History Sourcebook: England, India, and The East Indies, 1617 A.D." http://www.fordham.edu/halsall/india/1617englandindies.html.

CHAPTER 4

1. *Shorter Oxford English Dictionary*. New York: Oxford University Press, 2002, p. 2008.
2. Beeching, pp. 27–28.
3. Ibid., p. 28.
4. Spence, p. 129.

CHAPTER 5

1. Beeching, p. 25.
2. Ibid., p. 34.
3. Ibid.
4. Spence, p. 149.
5. Beeching, p. 43.
6. Ibid.
7. Ibid., p. 45.
8. Ibid.
9. Ibid., p. 46.
10. Ibid., p. 47.
11. Ibid., p. 48.
12. Ibid.
13. Ibid., p. 49.
14. Ibid.
15. Ibid., p. 50.
16. Ibid.

17. Ibid.
18. Ibid., p. 53.
19. Ibid.
20. Ibid., p. 62.

CHAPTER 6
1. Beeching, p. 67.
2. Ibid., p. 68.
3. Ibid., pp. 73–74.
4. Spence, p. 151.
5. Beeching, pp. 75–76.
6. Spence, p. 152.
7. Ibid., pp. 152–153.

CHAPTER 7
1. Beeching, p. 63.
2. Spence, pp. 153–154.
3. Ibid., p. 154.
4. Fay, p. 174.
5. Beeching, p. 92.
6. Spence, pp. 155–156.
7. Beeching, p. 110.
8. Ibid., p. 111.

9. Ibid., p. 113.
10. Spence, p. 156.
11. Beeching, p. 131.
12. Ibid., p. 130.
13. Spence, p. 157.
14. Beeching, p. 152.

CHAPTER 8
1. Beeching, p. 153.
2. Spence, p. 158.
3. Ibid., p 159.
4. Ibid.
5. Ibid.
6. Ibid.
7. Ibid.
8. Ibid., p. 160.
9. Ibid.
10. Ibid.
11. Ibid., p. 161.
12. Immanuel C.Y. Hsü, *The Rise of Modern China*, 6th ed., New York: Oxford University Press, 2000, p. 219.

BIBLIOGRAPHY

Beeching, Jack. *The Chinese Opium Wars*. New York: Harcourt Brace Jovanovich, 1975.

"China: Evolution of Foreign Policy," U.S. Library of Congress. Available online. URL: http://countrystudies.us/china/123.htm.

Chun, Wei. *On Ricci's Fallacies to Deceive the World*. Quoted in George H.C. Wong, "China's Opposition to Western Science During Late Ming and Early Ch'ing," *Isis* 54, No. 1. (March 1963).

"East India Company," Microsoft Encarta Online Encyclopedia 2008.

"The East India Company." Manas: History and Politics, East India Company. Available online. URL: http://www.sscnet. ucla.edu/southasia/History/British/EAco.html.

Fay, Peter Ward. *The Opium War: 1840–1842*. New York: W.W. Norton, 1975.

Hsü, Immanuel C.Y. *The Rise of Modern China*, 6th ed. New York: Oxford University Press, 2000.

"India History Sourcebook: England, India, and the East Indies, 1617 A.D." Available online. URL: http://www.fordham.edu/halsall/india/1617englandindies.html.

Lovell, Julia. *The Great Wall: China Against the World, 1000 BC–AD 2000*. New York: Grove Press, 1975.

"The Ming Dynasty's Maritime History." The Applied History Research Group / The University of Calgary. Available online. URL: http://www.ucalgary.ca/applied_history/tutor/eurvoya/ming.html.

Shorter Oxford English Dictionary. New York: Oxford University Press, 2002.

Spence, Jonathan D. *The Search for Modern China*. New York: W.W. Norton, 1990.

Waley, Arthur. *The Opium War Through Chinese Eyes*. London: Allen & Unwin, 1958.

Yun, Tan Mei. "Chinese Reactions to British Influence: Varying Chinese Views of the British." February 10, 2003. Available online. URL: http://www.angelfire.com/ny5/h3gproj/barbarians.htm.

FURTHER RESOURCES

Booth, Martin. *Opium: A History*. New York: St. Martin's, 1996.

Morris, James. *Farewell the Trumpets: An Imperial Retreat*. New York: Harcourt, Inc., 1978.

———. *Pax Britannica: Climax of an Empire*. New York: Harcourt, Inc., 1968.

Morris, Jan. *Heaven's Command: An Imperial Progress*. New York: Harcourt, Inc., 1973.

Spence, Jonathan D. *Return to Dragon Mountain: Memories of a Late Ming Man*. New York: Penguin, 2007.

———. *The Chan's Great Continent: China in Western Minds*. New York: W.W. Norton & Company, 1999.

PICTURE CREDITS

PAGE

 9: Hulton Archive/Getty Images

11: The Art Archive/Eileen
  Tweedy

23: The Granger Collection

26: The Art Archive/British
  Library

31: The Art Archive

35: The Art Archive/Marine
  Museum Stockholm/Alfredo
  Dagli Orti

41: Faculte de Pharmacie, Paris,
  France/Archives Charmet/
  The Bridgeman Art Library

46: The Granger Collection

57: The Granger Collection

65: Snark/Art Resource, NY

69: The Granger Collection

75: © Wolfgang Kaehler/CORBIS

85: The Granger Collection

89: Hulton Archive/Getty Images

93: AFP/Getty Images

96: © Infobase Learning

104: © Bettmann/CORBIS

INDEX

ABOUT THE AUTHOR

DENNIS ABRAMS is the author of numerous books for Chelsea House, including biographies of Barbara Park, Anthony Horowitz, Victor Yushchenko, Ty Cobb, Xerxes, Rachael Ray, Sandra Day O'Connor, Georgia O'Keeffe, and Hillary Rodham Clinton. He attended Antioch College where he majored in English and Communications. He lives in Houston, Texas, with his partner of 21 years, two cats, and a dog named Junie B.